THE **ULTIMATE** GUIDE TO A
DIGITAL WORKFORCE
EXPERIENCE

THE **ULTIMATE** GUIDE TO A
DIGITAL WORKFORCE
EXPERIENCE

LEAP FOR A PURPOSE

JASON AVERBOOK

Printed in the United States of America

Library of Congress Control Number: 2018946500

ISBN Paperback: 978-1-947341-23-4
ISBN eBook: 978-1-947341-22-7

Cover Design: Michelle Manley
Interior Design: Ghislain Viau

Contents

Foreword

For the past few years, I have been traveling the globe, working with HR leaders as well as delivering keynotes in virtually every part of the world. One of the blessings of being able to collaborate with people from every corner of the world is that you begin to see patterns and trends on a global basis before others. I had been collecting a ton of valuable insights that I had been sharing over and over again. One day, after speaking with the Chief HR Officer from one of the largest companies in the world, who had just finished reading my last book, *HR From Now to Next*, I realized that I needed to get the next set of important information out of my head, into a single body of work that could be shared, so I started writing immediately. Welcome to *The Ultimate Guide to A Digital Workforce Experience; Leap for a Purpose.*

I have come to a stark realization that we are at the moment in time that only occurs once every few decades when it comes to the combination of innovation and business readiness to push forward change that drives real value. This moment in time is probably best known as the Digital Workforce Experience Revolution.

For the past thirty years, the world of HR technology has been best defined just the way it sounds: technology that was purely designed to support the HR department. Today's workforce is one that is more global; more remote, with higher expectations; and, most importantly, chock full of digital natives who are used to being "serviced" through digital means versus waiting for humans to respond to their requests.

This book was written to help leaders in any size organization realize how to move from where they are now on their HR technology journey to how to create a vision and strategy to focus on workforce experience first and come to the realization that by doing so, the HR function will benefit with better data, more engaged employees, and, most importantly, a direct channel to deliver capabilities to the workforce now and into the future.

There is a brilliant quote from Jack Welch that reads: "If the rate of change on the outside exceeds the rate of change on the inside, then the end is near." We have reached that point where our workforce has better experiences in almost all aspects of their life than what we provide them at work, as far as getting things done in an experiential and natural manner. This can no longer be accepted, as it will drive engagement continuously lower, as well as lower the productivity of this workforce drastically. When it comes to the HR function, most of us are drastically behind the eight-ball by only continuing to automate existing processes in new technology versus really digitizing and reimaging. This has reached a crisis point, and our time is now to fix it.

We live in a world today that requires everyone in the HR function to have a "digital first" mentality. This does not mean we throw a bunch of technology against the wall and hope it sticks; what it means is that we must have a combination of a growth mindset, a workforce, and executives who believe digital transformation is key to the ongoing growth of the organization, and the ability to reimagine our old-fashioned HR processes leveraging design thinking to truly put the workforce at the center of our design versus our old way of doing things; focusing on HR requirements.

Each chapter of this book is written to guide you through the process of learning from the sins of the past, creating your new vision and strategy, learning how to execute on that strategy, and, finally, how to sustain your strategy and vision now and into the future. Deep value comes from focusing on continuous improvement and driving the workforce from a mentality of adoption to a cadence of addiction, and the only way to do that is to take the actions from this book, the take-aways at the end of each chapter, and put those into action in a strategic, "what fits for your organization" kind of manner.

I dedicate this book to all of my colleagues in the HR, IT, and business worlds that influence and guide my thinking on a continual basis. The collaboration of many is what drives the world forward, and this "piece of art" is a result of the brilliant ideas of those not afraid to change the world and make a difference now and into the future.

I want to thank my beautiful wife Heather for all of her ongoing support and my two "digital natives"—Ben, 13 years old, and Alex, 10 years old—for continuing to teach me how the world of work will "work" into the future, without even knowing the impact they have on my thinking. We all need to open our eyes and watch these digital natives, as they will create the workforce of the future, and if we do not act today, we will drastically disappoint them and let them down. Ben and Alex, I never want to disappoint you, and I hope that this book drives businesses around the world to create a world of work that will welcome you with open arms.

There has never been a time in my quarter century in this space where the concept of a growth mindset is so readily accepted by executives around the world, our workforce is ready to act digitally, our processes are begging and demanding to be reimagined, and the technology is ready to fuel our strategy. It truly is the most exciting time to be in this industry, and our time is now. I hope you enjoy my second book and think of it as another important infusion of knowledge as we continue, as a community, to make the world a better place. —*Jason Averbook*

1

Setting the Stage

Y ou can hardly believe your luck, but you've made it: you've been hired for a prime position in one of the world's most profitable, forward-thinking firms. Today is the start of the next chapter in your career.

Sweeping your first-day jitters aside, you take one last look in the bathroom mirror before you enter the office. Straighten your collar, smooth a couple of wrinkles out of your shirt—you look sharp! You've got that bright-eyed look of someone on the verge of something new and exciting. Your colleagues will adore you. Your bosses will be dazzled. You're ready to dive in.

As you pass through the frosted-glass double doors into the pristine office lobby, the chipper HR rep greets you warmly and leads you to her office. "Just a bit of paperwork to take care of first as we get you on board," she says. You'd like to meet your new colleagues first, but you know the drill.

You take a seat, and she whistles. A pair of guys in overalls wheel in a stack of eight hundred documents sitting atop a pallet. They drop the pile neatly on the desk in front of you.

"If you need anything, I'll be down the hall," the HR rep says brightly. She hands you a shiny new ballpoint pen and closes the door behind her.

Print your first and last name. Current address. Date of birth. Sign this, date that. Here's an I-9, a W-4, a bunch of documents allowing you to work outside of the United States, and we don't know what the hell this tax form is exactly, but why don't you fill it in anyway? Read this forty-three-page document on how to operate your office key card. Now specify your blood type. Favorite food. Name of your childhood dog. Your dog's blood type.

You sigh as you dutifully ink in the names and addresses of your last three employers. Didn't you already do this when you applied? You look out the window and you begin judging the "digital experience." The leaves are turning brown and falling from the trees. You write down your bank info for direct deposit. The first snow of the season blankets the earth. It's the holidays. You think of your family and wonder how they're doing. You wish you could see them, but you're only on page 443. Maybe you could call them. You close your eyes and strain to remember their phone number. Fortunately, it's in your emergency contact form, which you've filled out a dozen times already.

You keep writing. It's New Year's Eve. The night-shift janitor comes by and sings "Auld Lang Syne" to you. You read and sign a primer on "office norms." The sun streams through the window, warming your back. The daffodils bloom, lifting their yellow faces to the sun. You realize as you write down your date of birth for the eighth time that it is, in fact, your birthday today. The chipper HR rep knocks twice on the door frame and says, "Hey! There's cake in the break room. Come grab a piece when you're done! Sorry, the cake is gone!"

The days grow long and hot. You spot Fourth of July fireworks on the horizon. You're almost done with these documents. You shake your ballpoint pen to get the ink flowing. What was the job you applied for again? It's hard to remember.

The company has been sold. It's a new company now. Your new boss is a robot and he wants to know why you haven't finished your onboarding docs yet.

The chipper HR rep returns. "How are we doing here?" she asks.

"I'll be finished soon," you whisper. "I just need to read and sign these four pages about time-sheet protocol."

"OK, great! When you're all done, I'll take you to your desk and you can key all this info into the database!"

You squint and look up into the greenish glare of the fluorescent lights. A robot takes your job. The end. Welcome aboard!

* * *

Chances are, at some point, you've been there: excited to show up to a new job and dive in, only to have your enthusiasm deflated by a frustrating, redundant onboarding procedure that already has you wondering whether your employer really has it together.

Or maybe the Day 1 stuff goes smoothly, but the organization has a byzantine leave policy you can't make heads or tails of. Maybe no one in the human resources department is available when you need them most, or a simple home-address change involves more red tape than Soviet-era bureaucracy. Too many workplaces are plagued by such HR headaches, and although they're usually just a minor annoyance, over time, they take their toll. Individually, they can dampen an employee's mood or distract from work, or what we in HR call "engagement." On an organizational level, they can tarnish the corporate culture or chip away at workforce morale.

But it doesn't have to be that way. In fact, it *can't* continue to be that way. The world of HR needs to change to keep pace with how digital and mobile technologies have remade society and altered the way people interact with their world. The ease, speed, and convenience with which such technologies allow us to get what we want, when we want it, have raised the bar and changed expectations. Whether searching for information, purchasing a product, or completing a task, we want everything to be fast, personalized, data-driven, user-friendly, on-demand, and accessible anywhere—and we are less forgiving of inefficiency and inconvenience than we once were. Human resource departments must embrace the trend, leveraging available technologies and rethinking calcified organizational processes to deliver a new kind of workforce experience that matches employee expectations.

Nowhere is this shift more evident than in the consumer realm, where shoppers demand the ease of experience that mobile and digital have made possible: a seamless path between product perusal, selection, and delivery, whether it's ordering a skip-the-line coffee on the Starbucks app, booking a week-long hotel stay with a few clicks or swipes, or enjoying a multitude of personalized movie choices available to stream anywhere, anytime.

What was just a few years ago considered cutting edge is now the status quo, and this kind of forward-thinking synchrony between process and technology is no longer optional; it's a prerequisite for survival. Anything less, and your target market starts looking to spend their cash elsewhere. Don't believe me? Why don't you call Blockbuster's 800 number and see if they have any DVDs of *Good Will Hunting* available for rent this weekend?

For those of us in the human resources field, the same pressures—and opportunities—that have shaken up so many other industries have come to our door. HR departments that grasp the value of the "digital workforce experience" and its role in keeping people happy, productive, and engaged will lead the charge into the future. Those that don't will find themselves woefully behind.

What Is the Digital Workforce Experience?

A frictionless workforce experience means providing the right product to the right people at the right moment through the right channel.

The world of digital is the "IV" that delivers that experience. It is the means by which we in the HR profession keep up with how people engage with the world, whether they're at work, at home, or at play.

Illustration 1: IV to the Workforce

But it's not just a matter of slapping some modern software on old problems and old habits. We need to think of technology as existing alongside *mindset*, *people* and *processes*—the three elements must exist symbiotically in a way that allows all of them to flourish. In this book, we'll keep coming back to this theme—and later, I'll share the magic formula for balancing mindset, people, processes, and technology in order to produce a frictionless digital workforce experience.

If You Want to Reach People, You Have to Speak Their Language

Another reason technology is not the quick-fix panacea that many firms want it to be is that our target audience has

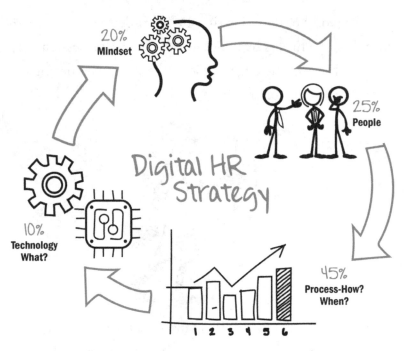

Illustration 2: Magic 20/25/45/10 Formula

changed. In the past, HR software was designed for use almost exclusively by HR professionals. The closest the average worker got to interacting with HR technology was when they'd call in to their human resources manager and hear them in the background tapping away at their keyboard.

Now, when we roll out a new piece of technology, the audience has flipped: 90 percent of the users are the employees and managers, and 10 percent are the HR departments. This means we have to redesign, and, most importantly, reimagine our processes for the end user, who is, in most cases, unfamiliar with the human resources profession, or even how to spell "HR."

But since we're also asking employees to do more (or at least, to do things differently), this also means we have to figure out how to get them to buy in. If we don't show them how a given piece of technology or a newfangled procedure makes their day easier and makes XYZ Inc. a more pleasant place to work, they're not going to use it.

Therefore, we have to change our messaging and marketing when we push it out to people. That means weaning ourselves off HR jargon and returning to the language of what biologists call "human beings." Individuals outside our industry don't speak "Payrollese." They don't know that the code for overtime is "OT8C," or that the "BAR Scale" is not a running list of after-work happy hours.

Here's another example: HR software often uses the term *effective date*, as in, "Martin is moving from Chicago to the Boise office. What is the effective date?" HR people know that the effective date might be the date that Martin moves, or it might be the date that happens to match a payroll cycle, or it may happen to be the date that matches when Martin's one-year benefits take effect, but its meaning is ambiguous for the average employee, for whom "effective date" is more likely to mean getting a good-night kiss or a next-day "I had a good time ;)" text.

Or consider that old HR stalwart, the Personnel Action Form, or PAF. Most large organizations still use some version of a PAF when managers need to transfer an employee internally.

Traditionally (and, in some cases, even now), this form was a piece of paper, often in triplicate, that would say something to the effect of, "Manny is transferring from Department A to Department B." Then you'd stick it in the interoffice mail and it would get routed to the appropriate people for approval. Eventually, it would make it back to HR, where you would formally apply that change, adding another week or two to the process.

Meanwhile, Manny has already started a new position in Department B, but it's not official because everyone has been waiting for this paperwork to go through. Poor Manny is caught in corporate limbo, which causes payroll problems and other issues. Now his manager has to get on the phone with HR and sort it out. But which manager? Department A's or Department B's?

Say Department A's manager takes the lead and makes the call, but gets no response. She calls back later, only to get rerouted to a different person, who promises to "look into it"—though probably not before he leaves for vacation at the end of the week. A simple problem becomes a multi-departmental entanglement. And on it goes, and it gets worse by the day.

This is the kind of problem the digital workforce experience seeks to resolve by taking old, impractical processes and using technology to reimagine them with a more "direct-access" approach. Now, instead of the manager having to print out, fill in, and mail the PAF to be handled by HR, there's one simple, self-explanatory, digitized form and process that the manager can do himself in a couple of minutes in order to make Manny's transfer official instantaneously.

Now, the aforementioned manager of Department A—let's call him Frank—is old school and tech averse. He held on to his typewriter until well into the Clinton administration. On interstate road trips, he uses actual maps to navigate. He made his wife return the Alexa she'd bought because he "didn't need another mouth to feed." And, as a long-time veteran of the company, he's been dealing with PAFs for nearly his whole career. It's the only way he knows.

People tend to resist change, and that's one of the impediments we HR folk face when we try to introduce new ways of doing things in order to perfect the digital workforce experience.

So how do we sell a guy like Frank on these changes? We have to *market* it to them by emphasizing the WIIFM: the "what's in it for me." Frank may be old-fashioned, but like anyone, he is in favor of anything that lightens his load. You get people on board when you can show them that they no longer have to fill out forms and play phone tag with the HR desk just to get a simple task done; now they have all the necessary tools at their disposal, at the click of a button.

You might be saying, "This seems like a *ton* of work, teaching all kinds of new processes and convincing our already busy workforce to buy in." And you're right; it is hard, at least at first. But there is a lot in it for you, the HR professional. A true ability to show empathy is key. For one thing, once employees and managers learn to use these tools, it reduces *your* workload and frees you to focus on those tasks that technology isn't so good at. Furthermore, the digitization of the HR function will generate a wealth of accurate, timely, granular data that you can harness to continually refine how you serve the organization, allowing the digital workplace experience to take root.

Don't Just "Lift and Shift"—*Transform*

Unfortunately, for many HR departments, the message is not getting through, even when they think it is. I often see HR professionals make the mistake of taking a woefully inefficient process and putting it online instead of changing it. "Look!" they exclaim. "Now our tedious, poorly functioning payroll system that's been causing biweekly emotional breakdowns for years is in the cloud!"

It's not enough to merely move broken processes and broken data onto a shiny new technology. That's just slapping a digital veneer onto mainframe-era thinking. It might yield a modicum of improvement, but nothing really gets solved; in fact, the problem becomes even more entrenched, because now your organization has spent the last six months rolling out an expensive new system that it's stuck with for the foreseeable future.

I describe this as the difference between *automation* and *digitization*. Automation, in this context, means taking an old, suboptimal process and "lifting and shifting" it onto an online format. It might be a step in the right direction, but it's not a *transformation* of old habits. Digitization, in contrast, means truly reimagining a process in a way that adds value for HR personnel, staff, management, and everyone else.

On this point, we can again look to the consumer sector for inspiration. Take Starbucks, which reimagined the whole process of buying coffee with its "Mobile Order & Pay" app. By ordering and paying on your phone, you can just waltz into the store, breeze up to the counter, and pick up your order, which has already been prepared for you by the time you walk through the door. The experience is a pleasant one, free of the loathsome hassle of waiting in line.

The "Mobile Order & Pay" app has been a resounding success for Starbucks, but the company is continuing to make the experience even more seamless by adding text and voice-command functionality to its interface. The best part is that everyone benefits: the baristas' workload is reduced because they no longer have to swipe credit cards and count change, the customers get in and get out more quickly, and the company profits from the efficiency. It's a fine example of mindset, people, process, and technology coming together in a frictionless fashion. HR leaders, take note.

Illustration 3: Starbucks "Mobile Order & Pay" App

Or consider Manny's PAF fiasco we talked about earlier. Most organizations would just apply "lift and shift" thinking to the issue and take the old PAF form and put it online—but still make managers go through the rigmarole of printing it, sending it through the interoffice mail system, etc. And woe unto you if you forget to sign it! Then it'll be another week of waiting before it comes back to you with a note that says, "The legal department says we need your signature, no exceptions." Meanwhile, the rest of the world is using DocuSign or some other electronic signature tool. That is what we mean by automating something but failing to take it to that next level by truly digitizing it.

What's at Stake?

As I mentioned in the Foreword, Jack Welch, former CEO of General Electric, once said, "If the rate of change on the outside exceeds the rate of change on the inside, the end is near." We've seen this play out time and again: many of the biggest household names in the corporate world have succumbed to external changes they just couldn't keep up with, or chose not to. Now those firms are a punch line or a cautionary tale in an MBA class: think of Blockbuster's colossal failure to catch on to DVD-by-mail and streaming video, or of Kodak clinging stubbornly to film, even as digital photography (a technology Kodak basically invented) was permanently overtaking the market.

We might think that within the cozy confines of the HR department, we're insulated from such competitive pressures, but that's not the case. HR must take a lead role in spurring innovation, change, and growth. We can't afford to remain static while the outside world is evolving at breakneck speed.

It's an HR axiom that a company's most valuable asset is its workforce (although, truthfully, I've worked with firms where it'd be fair to say the most valuable asset was the Keurig machine). If the day-to-day experience at work is unpleasant, productivity suffers, morale declines, and employees defect to greener pastures. Therefore, it's no exaggeration to say when we talk about the digital workforce experience that the profitability and survival of the company itself are at stake.

And we don't have much time to get up to speed. In the information economy, the rate of change is ever-increasing— blink and you can get left in the dust. Given that it takes a year, two years, or longer to execute major programs, the time to get started is now. Only in this way can we meet the demands of a brave new labor market head-on.

It's a tall order, but with the right vision and the right mindset, it can be done. The next chapters will show you how.

TAKEAWAYS

1. **Don't move forward until you realize a digital workforce experience is more than just HR technology.**

   We live in a world today where the expectations of the workforce have never been higher. They have better technology and experiences in the palm of their hand than they receive in their place of employment. We can no longer stand up HR systems and hope they provide an experience. We truly need to create a digital workforce experience strategy now.

2. **Speak the language of the people.**

   Just like most of us, the workforce was not raised to work in HR. Most employees don't understand HR terms, they don't understand why HR exists, and most don't even know what the vision of the HR function is. They understand the work they have been hired to do and that they are passionate about. That means we in HR can no longer speak to the workforce in terms such as time-to-fill, self-service, LMS, ATS, or earnings code. We all have our own lens as to the language we relate to, and HR must relate to the common workforce, not those few employees with HR know-how.

3. **Our time is now! LEAP!**

   There has never been a point in time in the history of the HR automation/digitization era where things have been aligned as well as they are today. The people are ready with a new mindset to work differently, and not only are they ready, they expect it. The processes we use to get work done are dated, but there are tools and thought processes today to help us reimagine how people services are delivered and how work gets done. Finally, the technology is here today to truly transform how we serve and communicate to the workforce: with purpose, with integrity, and with value to change the function forever. The stakes are high, and our time must be now!

Where Things Go Wrong

Many factors might impede a company's efforts to develop a strong workforce experience, but three in particular consistently knock things off track: lack of vision; the "strategy-deployment chasm"; and emphasizing technology over mindset, people, and processes.

Your Vision and Mindset: What Do You Want to Be?

It might seem intuitive to have an overall strategy before pressing ahead, but you'd be surprised at how many organizations do things without really considering the bigger picture of *why* they're doing them. It's the strategic equivalent of "leaping before you look." You can't just buy technologies or implement processes without a clear vision of who you are and where you want to go as an organization. If you skip this step and dive headfirst into execution mode, it won't matter if you have the best people working around the clock—all your efforts to develop that digital workforce experience will be for naught.

Often, when I ask about vision, people say, "Well, we have a project plan," or maybe, "I've got an implementation partner who's overseeing how to put this technology in place." But a vision is broader, more overarching, more all-encompassing, and more strategic. It's something that is connected with an organization's core objectives, its mission, and its values. These elements are the organization's "signature": who we are, what we stand for, how we are unique, and what we hope to become.

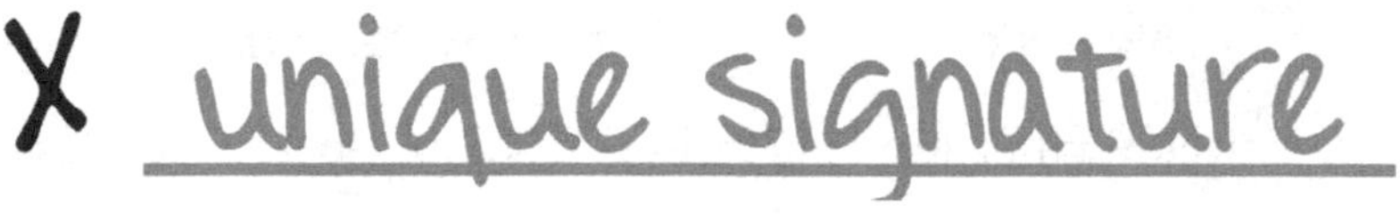

✗ _unique signature_

Illustration 4: Unique Signature and DNA

Since a vision encompasses the goals and values of the organization as a whole, it stands to reason that the vision must be shared organization-wide. It can't just be something cooked up by one or two people at the top; it must be the product of a cross-functional group that includes HR, IT, the C-suite, and the employees engaged in the actual business (with representatives from different lines of business).

Without the input and collaboration of multiple departments, you just end up with a hodgepodge of competing voices, individual projects, and varying, sometimes divergent goals. That said, it's not always easy to bridge these departmental gaps—even if you lock everyone in a room together and don't let them out until they come up with a plan. That's why the leadership of the HR department is so vital in energizing the process and mobilizing stakeholders. Because HR, by nature, should be knowledgeable about all facets of an organization, it is uniquely suited to breaking down the various silos and pulling them all together. Of course, human resources has its own intradepartmental silos, so you must be mindful of getting those parts to move in sync as well.

No Vision without a Vision Statement

A vision is not just a nebulous assemblage of nice ideas that float somewhere up in the clouds. It must take concrete, actionable form as a *vision statement*, which should be powerful, concise, precise, and unambiguous. It should be large enough to convey the aspirations of the whole organization, but compact enough to be articulated in just a few phrases—the elegant brevity of the classic thirty-second elevator pitch.

The vision statement should also be *challenging*. It has to push the organization forward. It can't be something pedestrian, like, "Our vision is to be able to keep bread on the table." It should inspire the workforce to excel and make employees excited to be a part of it.

I like to think of the vision statement as a set of guardrails. By definition, guardrails are a barrier—but one that furthers progress rather than hindering it. Think of the guardrails on the highway. In one respect, they are limiting: you can't just jerk the wheel and go off-roading on a whim (although, admittedly, there are days when that is tempting). But guardrails are also a mechanism that facilitates the highway's proper function, directing the flow of traffic and enabling us to get where we're going safely and efficiently. The vision statement works the same way: guiding you on a clear path toward your destination.

We Have Our Vision—Now What?

The vision statement is not just a pretty-sounding tagline to put at the beginning of annual reports, wedged between the table of contents and the acknowledgments nobody reads. It must influence the day-to-day behavior of everyone from the CEO to the interns, and any person in the organization should be able to recite it. We want the vision to be short and sweet because the goal is for it to become embedded in the DNA of the organization—living, breathing, and ever present.

Your vision statement must also be dynamic. A great vision is in "perpetual beta." It's not just something organizations do once, then put it in a box and say, "OK, done with the vision! What's next on the list?" You must have a hand in its conception and implementation, and you must actively promote it.

Of course, that's easier said than done. How do we prevent the vision statement from being relegated to an inspirational poster in the break room or the restroom? How do we incorporate it into the organization's DNA?

The key is marketing. HR professionals love talking about change management, but our approach to change management also needs to be rethought. Until now, we've mostly handled it as a matter of *training*—"I have to train my people in this new process/system/software." Instead, we should think of it as *marketing*—how do we "market" change measures to our workforce so they remember, believe, and buy in?

Marketing is how you get the vision of the digital workforce experience into the very fabric of the organization, making it an organic part of people's daily lives, and not just an afterthought.

Marketing may be a new thing to many HR professionals. For decades, our outlook has been insular: HR people doing HR functions. But our target market has changed. Even the very phrase *target market* is . . . well, a marketing term.

It's a novel approach, but it needn't be complicated. It just means we need to meet people where they are. Say you're rolling out an employee wellness initiative featuring a tool that tracks weight loss, blood pressure, and other health metrics. But instead of debuting it in connection with the vision statement, you just present it as a stand-alone feature called "My Health," without emphasizing the link to the broader organizational strategy. People aren't going to grasp its significance, and they may not even use it.

That's a missed opportunity. Tie everything back to the vision. Drive the point home.

Proof statements are another effective way of making the vision permanent, inspirational, and real. Visions, as I said before, are based on goals, and goals should be measurable. If you can demonstrate concrete evidence of progress, you reinforce the perception of the vision as an actionable, living, breathing thing that is having an impact.

Remember that people don't just show up at work to get a paycheck. That may be the main reason they get out of bed in the morning, but that's not really what *drives* them. The happiest workers and the most vibrant organizations do more than just make money: they produce something meaningful, and they add value to their industry or sector, or even to the world at large. And employees derive satisfaction from being part of that. Marketing the vision and its attendant progress helps cultivate a love affair with the business as an organization that *matters*.

Unfortunately, most organizations are not doing *any* of this work of pushing out and marketing the vision. The prevailing attitude seems to be, "OK, here it is. We'll put it out there, and if people don't consume it or practice it, that's their fault." That's the worst possible way to think. The burden is on us to earn their buy-in, even if that means hitting people over the head with it in almost every communication until the workforce doesn't just know it, but *lives* it.

The Strategy-Deployment Chasm

Picture yourself standing on the edge of a gorge and gazing across its expanse. You're on the strategy side. On the other side of the gap lies the deployment side. The rocky canyon in between is what I call the strategy-deployment chasm, that dreaded abyss into which many organizations fall when they try to move from one side to the other. In my experience, about 80 percent of organizations suffer this fate by failing to execute the strategy they've conceived.

Several factors account for this problem. Companies simply forget about their vision almost as soon as they've created it. They've articulated a perfect vision statement, fine-tuned it with input from all the major departments, and are ready to roll it out to great fanfare.

Illustration 5: Strategy Deployment Chasm

Then the implementation phase arrives, and just as quickly, the vision falls by the wayside. All the laminated copies, the professionally designed posters, and the slick marketing materials are nowhere to be found. Or they debut it, but the employees don't seem to care one way or the other—they're just trying to finish that day's project, clock out, and go home to binge on Netflix.

Execution failure can also occur when the executives and other organization leaders who crafted the vision aren't part of its deployment.

Imagine you've hired an architect to build you a house. "What kind of house?" the architect says.

"Oh, you know, a housey house," you say. "With, like, a living room, a couple of bedrooms, and a kitchen. OK? Call me in six months when you've finished!"

That's a rather vague description of a home, and its final form could end up looking fifty different ways—especially if you bow out during the execution phase. But that kind of disconnect frequently exists among HR, IT, and other departments involved in building the digital workforce experience. You have to be engaged in the build itself; otherwise, the end result may not be what you envisioned.

I've seen it happen many times: Once the vision is launched, the higher-ups pass the baton to the tactical people in the organization. But if the tactical people weren't involved in creating the vision, or if no one has conveyed to them how important it is, it can become just one of a dozen things on their weekly to-do list.

You can guess what happens next. Say you're installing a piece of HR technology in pursuit of this grand new workforce experience. The IT people will say to the software vendor, "Well, we usually do things this way," without even thinking about the organizational strategy.

Or they may be dimly aware of that strategy, but they haven't been given any concrete guidance on what to do with it. So they say to the vendor, "We're not sure what exactly the executives had in mind, and it's going to be six weeks before we can sit down with them, so let's just go with what we already know." In other words, the culture of doing the same.

In this case, the IT people are just following the path of least resistance, which usually means "the less change, the better." They're automating, but they're not digitizing; they're lifting and shifting, not creating something altogether different and visionary. In the end, what gets deployed is more or less the same as what the organization has been doing for years. There's no change.

Here's a real-life example: The HR department of a medium-sized firm was developing a new portal with all the information employees needed to do their jobs effectively, with a single click or single touch. That was what they envisioned, at least.

To implement this idea, they hired a group of third-party developers. Those developers received only basic, nuts-and-bolts instructions. They didn't understand the vision, weren't involved in its conception, weren't part of the organization, and effectively had no stake in the company's strategic future. All they were given was what the company stipulated in the requirements document, which was that the portal had to be simple, intuitive, and easy to use.

Now, what's easy to use, simple, and intuitive to a developer is completely different from what's easy to use, simple, and intuitive to a worker who uses this tool once a month. An employee wants to navigate by using a search bar or by talking into their smartphone, using natural language processing, à la Siri or Alexa. But that's not how developers like to search.

Or say your organization has a sizable number of employees who are color-blind. That's obviously an important design concern if you're creating an experience that's simple and user-friendly. There might also be Americans with Disabilities Act stipulations to adhere to. But developers don't think in those terms. Consequently, a lot of essential things get left out, and what you get might be different from your vision; it might even be a little better, but it's not "visionary"—it doesn't support any kind of long-term strategic objective for the workforce experience.

For this reason, the executives who helped create the vision must continue to have a hand in its deployment. Otherwise, into the chasm you go!

The last reason for falling into the strategy-deployment chasm is that, as I mentioned before, our target market is completely different now. The building of a digital workforce experience involves technologies and processes that are designed for the workforce at large, rather than for HR insiders. This means that you can't take their buy-in for granted: If they don't like, can't figure out, or fail to grasp the utility of a process or technology, they're not going to use it. If the WIIFM (what's in it for me) isn't evident, you'll lose them.

For example, imagine you're debuting a new employee database system that conveniently stores everything under one digital roof: name, address, department, where they attended school, the names of their kids, etc. After much time and effort computerizing reams of data, you introduce the system to the workforce. But when Joe Employee uses this highly touted, newfangled system, he just sees a lot of blank fields where the corresponding information should be—big, glaring, white gaps.

That's when Joe turns to his cube mate and scoffs, "*This* is what HR has been working on for the last six months? They may as well have given us a pen and a stack of triplicate forms with carbon paper." I like making people laugh as much as the next guy, but believe me, being the water cooler joke du jour is not the kind of workforce experience we're aiming for.

Nor will it make any difference if your rollout is just the first stage of a multiphase project, and you promise everyone that Phase 2 and Phase 3 will correct these shortcomings. At that point, it doesn't matter if your vision is stellar, you've met all your deadlines, and the next phase is going to achieve everything you dreamed it would. You've already lost your audience. They're not going to stick around for "Phase N" ("N" for *never*) while you get it together.

Phase I...Phase N

Illustration 6: Phase 1 Must Add Value

If you don't believe me, think about the way consumers engage with digital products. If you buy a smartphone app that's buggy, inadequate, or poorly designed, you're going to delete it immediately, and you're not going to check back later to see if there's an update. No one ever says, "Hey, remember that awful photo editor app I downloaded six months ago and then promptly uninstalled? I wonder what their dev team is up to! Let's see if version 2.0 is out yet!"

Granted, the context of this analogy is a little different, because at work, employees don't have the same range of consumer choice. But we can't just act as if HR has cornered the market. We may not be competing with other apps, but we *are* competing with "the old way of doing things" as we strive to get our workforce to use the new technologies we push out to them. And the old way of doing things has a lot of sway—especially if it works better than the new way.

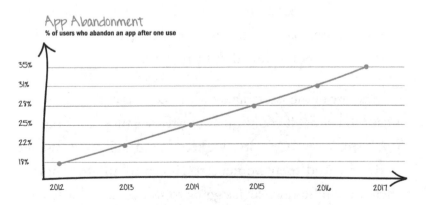

Illustration 7: Abandonment of Apps

31

Emphasizing Technology over Mindset, People, and Processes

One of the more consistent sources of amusement in my life is watching people watch software demos. It's like they've had a glimpse of nirvana. "If only I had that, everything would be perfect!" Call it Shiny Object Syndrome—the impulse to latch on to a nice-looking product without considering whether and at what cost it can be integrated with your own needs, or how it fits into your workforce experience strategy.

Everything looks great on the showroom floor, but when it's time to implement it, you sometimes discover that adapting a piece of software to your particular needs calls for so much tweaking that the solution no longer has that same easy, breezy thrill it offered in the demo.

Shiny Object Syndrome highlights a bigger reason things go wrong when we try to create a great digital workforce experience: an overemphasis on technology as the means to an end. Technology is obviously a critical part of everything we do in HR. but it shouldn't be the *focus*.

The rise of the "software as a service" has changed things. It used to be that if you wanted to license a program, your IT people would say, "OK, first, we need to order all our computer hardware. And then we need to find a room at corporate where we can fit it, where it's going to stay cool, and where it's secure," and so on. Then those same IT people would make sure that you could actually run databases on that machine and keep it healthy.

In short, it was a lot of work. Deploying technology meant you would have 50, 60, or even 70 percent of your resources concentrated on IT. It was like having a baby, so exhausting that by the time you finished, you would collapse and say, "Oh my God. Seriously, I can't do that again!" But at least you knew that if the technology was working, everything else would fall into place.

Now, in the software-as-a-service era, it's the vendor who is handling the implementation grunt work. The vendor simply says, "Guys, all you need is a URL to be able to access your application, and it's ready to go." Maybe you need to tweak the security settings a bit, assess how multiple SaaS products might integrate, and personalize a few functions, but otherwise the work is done. You don't need a big IT team customizing it, implementing it, and managing it.

This is a boon for HR departments, since it means we can devote resources to other areas. But most organizations are still stuck in that old mindset—that 50 to 70 percent of time, energy, and manpower should be concentrated on the technology instead of on people and processes.

Creating a digital workforce experience flips the formula: Mindset, people, and process should now consume the bulk of your attention. The secret recipe is a 20/25/45/10 mix: 20

percent mindset, 25 percent people, 45 percent process, and 10 percent technology.

Twenty percent of your focus should start with a new mindset; which means striving to maintain a growth mindset: an openness to change, diversity of thought, and work differently. This focus will also mean communicating to others the importance of this new mindset shift. Twenty-five percent of your time should be dedicated to analyzing who will use the tools: understanding their desires, their dislikes, and what makes them tick. You must also identify the people who will make the decisions, those who will make up your governance council, and how will you get them on board with these changes.

Another 45 percent of your time will be invested in figuring out processes. Who do you want them to flow to? How do you want them to function in the structure of the organization? Which systems are they going to touch? How can you reimagine them to work with a new world of work and a new audience?

Then, once you've addressed mindset, people, and processes, the technology becomes the easy part, almost falling into place.

Nevertheless, old habits die hard. This is true of individuals and especially of organizations, where things are often the way they are simply because that's the way they always have been. It's hard to shake firms of their technology-centric mindset. "This is a technology project," they say. "It's not a workforce experience project or an HR project."

Yes, but who is the technology *for*? Who will be directly affected by the tech? The people! It only makes sense to approach it from this perspective.

TAKEAWAYS

1. Everything starts with a strategic vision.

Don't leap before you look: Articulate a succinct but compelling statement about who you want to be as an organization and where you want to go. Have it reflect your mission and values. Gather input from different departments, but make sure the final message is clear and cohesive. This vision will be the compass that guides your decisions going forward.

2. Launching the strategy is just the start.

You can't just create a strategy and set it loose into the wild. You must actively promote it until it becomes part of the organizational DNA. Executives must have a hand in its implementation and deployment. Think of it as being in perpetual beta: an ongoing process of tweaking and fine-tuning and continuing to gain buy-in every step of the way.

3. 20/25/45/10

These are the magic numbers for rolling out a digital workforce experience: focus 20 percent mindset, 25 percent people, 45 percent on processes, and 10 percent on technology.

What Have We Learned?

Bad things happen when the different parts of an organization act independently, without an overall strategy in place. You can't tango when everyone else is doing hip-hop. Everything must start with the strategy.

Not long ago, I dealt with a company whose HR division wanted to improve its workforce experience, but each department was doing its own thing. The recruiting department rolled out a tool they called "My Recruiting." The benefits department rolled out something they called "Benny." The learning department introduced "The Train" for training. The payroll department debuted something they called "Money."

Illustration 8: Benny

Each system had a different design, a different color, different branding, and a different way to navigate. In some cases, different tools provided the same information, performed the same tasks, or asked the same questions. In other cases, the information provided in one tool contradicted that given by another. All of them were awkward to use and bloated with HR jargon.

In short, it was a confusing, unworkable spaghetti of systems, processes, brands, and design schemes, and the employees for whom it was intended did not like it. They barely even used it. It was easier to call someone or ask the person sitting in the next cube.

Without a holistic vision, all the different HR silos won't communicate with one another. Employees don't want to work for that kind of firm. They want a seamless experience in which each department can fulfill its respective duties while working in sync with all the other parts of the organization. You can see this for yourself by perusing reviews employees have left on Glassdoor. It's a sad compendium of employer errors, reported by people who are fed up with old technology, old processes, bad leadership, leaders not having access to data, and all the other factors that affect the daily experience at work.

Illustration 9: Call Someone

Before any HR leader spends money on new technologies, they should first think, "What is my digital strategy? How do I make sure that the organization has bought into that digital strategy? And how do I get the governance and process in place to make sure that I stick to that strategy on an ongoing basis?" Organizations that do this have a 90- to 95-percent chance of success at developing a great workforce experience. Those that don't will succeed maybe 5 percent of the time, and that success is usually short-lived.

Technology without Strategy: Putting the Digital Cart before the Horse

To get a sense of what happens when you start licensing costly technology without the guardrails of a strategic vision, consider the following story: the HR technology director of a West Coast firm became enamored with the use of natural language processing (NLP) for intelligent personal assistants like Siri or Alexa. Ask the device virtually any question, and it answers, often with an impressive degree of precision.

It *is* pretty amazing to think about the range of applications such technology could have for a data-centric profession like human resources, where so much of what we do involves answering questions and delivering information to people. With this technology, no longer does an employee have to type a query into a search bar. Now they can ask their own device about the company's vacation policy, or whether St.

Patrick's Day is a paid holiday, or how bad a hangover needs to be before they can qualify for a sick day.

It's a great idea, in theory—it's exactly the kind of change that we look for to develop a better workforce experience. The problem was that the director was not thinking about things holistically. Enchanted by the siren song of sexy new technology, he failed to consider how or whether it would function for *his* organization. The company's data storage and retrieval architecture was in disarray. Different policies were stored in different databases and administered by different HR personnel working in different silos. An employee could spend all day asking the AI program about vacation leave, but if that information wasn't centralized, retrievable, and stored in a format that could be integrated with the licensed software, it was useless. Shiny Object Syndrome had once again reared its sparkly, ugly head.

Illustration 10: Strategy Development

It helps to think of strategy development as a cyclical process, as in the above diagram. The strategy is the vision of where you want to go. The road map is a macro-level, years-long prescription for action. A plan is the more micro-level methodology for achieving the objectives of the road map. Plans comprise actions and resources needed—the concrete steps taken to move from concept to finished product.

Once you've completed the actions, you should measure the results and take account of your strategy's successes and failures, its strong points and its weak links. Armed with that information, you can re-evaluate and refine it, kicking off the process all over again.

Let's examine how this cycle works with a simple analogy. Imagine that you're overseeing an airport's air traffic, which is expected to grow in the next three years. There are eight gates and eight airlines that fly into the airport. Your strategy is to make sure the airport can accommodate the spike in traffic.

The road map says, "Over the next three years, here is what we need to do at a macro level to make that happen: there are eight gates, so we'll assign one airline to each gate, and make sure there aren't multiple flights arriving at a single gate at once." The road map is supported by the plan, which goes into more micro-level detail about how to accomplish that: basically, each individual gate constitutes a "plan." That plan gets even more granular when you look at the actions—designing the daily flight schedules, assigning different flights to different gates at different times, scheduling the personnel you need in the control tower and on the runway to make sure everything runs smoothly, and so forth.

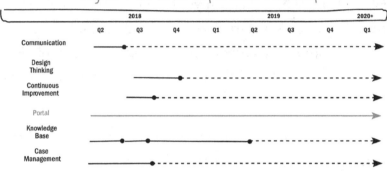

Illustration 11: Experience Roadmap

Following this kind of systematic schema for strategy helps you avoid Shiny Object Syndrome and other common pitfalls.

It's a Program, Not a Project

The "strategy cycle" is a particularly apt visual representation of the process involved in creating a workforce experience, because one of the defining features of that process is its continuity.

In the last chapter, we talked about the workforce experience program being in perpetual beta—undergoing a constant process of implementation, testing, measuring, revision, and improvement. It's living; it's breathing; it's constantly growing. There will always be changes. It never has an end date.

It's not just our profession. The whole world of business and technology is being reshaped by the digital economy, which has created an eternal state of flux. If we don't keep up, we'll fall behind. Therefore, creating a digital workforce experience is a *program*, not a project. Most organizations are still stuck in the old, myopic, project-oriented way of thinking: there's a start date, an end date, and a team of people temporarily tasked with bringing it to completion. Then, once it's over, all those people will be shifted onto the next project.

Programs are different. They have a start date, but no end date. They operate in perpetuity. They are agile at the core. The structure is different, too: a program often comprises a multitude of projects. While projects are more specialized, siloed, and "atomistic," programs are more generalized, inclusive, and holistic. With a program, the whole organization is involved. A digital workforce experience program depends on the involvement of and input from various departments to function frictionlessly. And it's always on.

Think of it like getting in shape: you can't just hit the gym a couple times and then say, "OK, done with that!" It's not even a matter of working out consistently until you can declare victory upon reaching your target weight, since we all know how quickly—as soon as you step off the scale, it seems—you gain back all the weight you just lost. Fitness is a continuous process that demands long-term lifestyle changes

Project

- Definition of specific project goals
- Intake and management of project requirements
- Breakdown and scheduling of tasks
- Budget and cost management
- Assignment and management of project resources
- Communication of project status against milestones

Program

- Prioritizing and funding initiatives over projects
- Defining and maintaining a cross-organizational roadmap
- Ensuring resource capacity and availability across enterprise
- Managing interdependencies between projects
- Ensuring that program-level goals are achieved

Illustration 12: Project vs. Program

and an ongoing retooling of your diet and exercise regimen. Building a workforce experience is the same (although thankfully with less Zumba).

The programmatic approach also means that the marketing never stops. In the previous chapter, we discussed how marketing is the means by which you initiate workforce experience changes into the workplace DNA. The marketing has to be widespread and persistent because it takes the buy-in of the organization as a whole to push these programs along, to make them permanent.

Marketing a workforce experience program is different from, say, marketing a movie. When a movie-marketing campaign begins, you see Vin Diesel brandishing cartoonishly large guns in front of a colorful CGI explosion for six weeks on every city bus and during every other commercial break. Then the release date comes, the film screens for a few weeks, and then Vin's bulging muscles are replaced by Ryan Gosling's smirk as the studio starts to promote the next blockbuster.

Marketing the digital workforce experience is more like the ad campaigns of GEICO, the auto insurance company: year after year, you hear the same slogan and see that same damn gecko. But something about it must be working, or they wouldn't still be doing it after all this time.

Perpetual. Never-ending. Always on. This kind of language can make HR employees shudder. After all, isn't that every office worker's worst nightmare—a Sisyphean labor that starts all over again as soon as you think you've achieved your goal?

Well, besides the fact that the work involved in developing a workforce experience is rewarding and—dare I say it?—*fun*, the beauty of it is that everything becomes easier over time. Perpetual beta doesn't mean you're going to be forever smoothing out the same kinks and troubleshooting the same rough spots. It means that after a while, your workforce begins to see, feel, and *experience* the positive changes and palpable benefits that you've been so diligently designing.

Once people start using these tools, the process of pushing it out to them becomes self-sustaining, and people no longer need to be told to use them; they just do it by habit. It evolves from being a massive change to just being "how we do things around here." Smooth. Natural. Part of the DNA.

Riding the Wave

One benchmark we can use for measuring how well we're adapting to the tidal wave of digital change is asking, "Is the experience we offer our employees as good as or almost as good as the experience we offer our customers?"

Think about how easy it is to order something on Amazon. Almost every conceivable consumer desire is available at the touch of a button: within literally sixty seconds, you can have your product of choice ordered and queued up for delivery.

Now imagine if you could browse online, but you couldn't order digitally. Imagine that you had to call up a sales rep, read out the product number digit by digit, give all your personal information over the phone (and God forbid you have a long address or a polysyllabic surname!), and then listen to hold music while the sales rep confirms your purchase.

Needless to say, it would make for a wholly unsatisfying consumer experience. Any company that tried to do business that way would fold within a month.

The implication for HR professionals is clear: if it doesn't work for retailers, it's only a matter of time before it becomes unsustainable for us. The standards have changed; employees' expectations are different. No longer are they going to put up with spending half their lunch break on the phone with HR to process a simple change of address form. In fact, on average, people in organizations waste 60 percent of their time doing things other than work. That is unacceptable to employees, to executives, to shareholders—to everyone.

If you don't have a strategy, if you're thinking of projects instead of programs, and if you're not actively making your vision part of the organizational DNA, you're going to end up developing processes that don't make sense and blowing your budget on technology that doesn't serve the needs of the workforce. Before you know it, you're out of funding, your credibility is shot because the results you've promised haven't been realized, and corporate is not going to indulge your next request for an expensive technological overhaul. Now you're basically stuck, putting the whole organization at risk. And in the worst case, you might be out of a job, relegated to the misery of Indeed.com, where you'll have to send out resumes to maddening companies whose job application forms make you type in your whole resume manually—before asking you to upload it on the very next page.

But not to worry, that's just the worst-case scenario. If you're reading this book, you're already aware of the stakes, and you have an idea of what needs to be done. The red-hot pace of digital means that we need to get on board immediately, but for those organizations that are doing so, the future looks bright.

The digital workforce experience offers us a once-in-a-generation opportunity to revitalize the entire human resources profession, and to permanently do away with fossilized approaches to work that have held us back for years. In the next chapter, we'll talk more about how to take what we've learned thus far and pull it all together to make this lofty ambition a reality.

TAKEAWAYS

1. **Start with a strategy.**

   The strategy bridges the gap between silos and provides a long-term vision to guide your actions. Create a road map for your strategy, a plan for your road map, and action items to execute the plan. Then evaluate your results and repeat the process.

2. **Beware of the Shiny Object Syndrome.**

   Impulse buying gets us into trouble—and when the product is expensive HR technology and the consumer is an entire organization, the harmful effect of buying the wrong thing is amplified. Don't be seduced by the allure of software that may not suit your needs.

3. **Think of programs, not projects.**

   Programs are ongoing and organization-wide, and a programmatic approach aligns with a perpetual beta design. But perpetual beta doesn't mean perpetual work. Eventually your efforts will achieve momentum, and what was once new and unfamiliar will become routine and automatic—part of the organization's DNA.

4

What Is a Workforce Experience?

One of the more interesting developments of the current era is that work is about a lot more than work. It's not just punching in, plugging through projects, putting out a certain product or service, punching out, and doing it all over again the next day.

Today, the scope of the workforce experience has expanded beyond an exclusive focus on "what you do" to take into consideration "how you feel." Human resources reflects that change, having evolved beyond a numbers-crunching, industrial approach in managing an organization's personnel to a more empathetic focus on the emotional content of each employee's day-to-day experience.

> Maya Angelou
> "I've learned that people will forget what you said, people will forget what you did, but people will never forget how you made them feel."

After all, one of our core objectives is to keep employees happy, that is, to make them feel good about coming to the office (or shoe store, or factory, or wherever they're employed) and the purpose of their role. We do this because we genuinely care about their well-being, and we do it because it's good for business. It's a well-known fact that happy workers are productive workers. And job satisfaction is the best defense against attrition.

A good workforce experience encompasses a lot of little things—how easy it is to park, who greets you at the front desk, how wide the menu options are at the cafeteria, whether diverse communities feel included and welcomed—all of which help answer the big question: "What is it like to work for this organization?"

In the last decade or so, a number of prominent companies (most notably Google) have generated headlines about their fun on-site perks. But Ping-Pong tables, free Belgian waffles, and employer-sponsored chair massages are only part of the equation, and providing them will make little difference if your workers lack the tools they need to get things done—especially administrative and HR-related tasks, which are not part of their normal job function and should therefore consume as little time as possible.

Fortunately, we don't have to reinvent the wheel: the digital consumer experience can serve as our benchmark for the next five to ten years. Is processing a pay raise as easy as ordering shrimp lo mein on Grubhub? Is the procedure for requesting an ergonomic chair as intuitive as calling a car on Lyft? Can shift-scheduling changes and leave requests be tracked in real time like a pizza delivery on the Domino's app?

The world has changed, and we need to change with it. The ease, speed, and convenience of digital have become ubiquitous in private life, which means that people expect such service all the time, everywhere, including at work. Thanks to their smartphones, employees are accustomed to having the entire world in the palms of their hands, and they don't want to blast back to 1998 the minute they enter the office. They want a frictionless experience—and it's up to HR to give it to them.

More than an Interface

Ride-sharing apps like Lyft and Uber have revolutionized the taxi industry and changed how people get from point A to point B. Technologically, they're a marvel; experientially, they're a breeze. But what happens if you order a Lyft to the airport, and en route the driver gets into an accident, and you miss your flight? What if you then discover that unbeknownst to the company, the driver's license has recently been suspended in the wake of a DUI?[1] Your day—and maybe your whole week—is ruined, and you surely won't think highly of Lyft after that. But that's not a technological flaw; it's a breakdown in process. Just having good technology is no guarantee of a good experience, even if the technology works as intended.

Or consider this: one of the secondary perks of ride-sharing apps is the human interaction they inspire between driver and passenger, the kind of momentary connection that elevates a ride to an experience. That can go in the opposite direction as well: sometimes, all you want to do is stare out the window for a few minutes and think about your evening plans, or maybe about nothing in particular. A chatty driver can spoil those few precious minutes of peace and silence.

---

1 It should be noted here that while this scenario is not *impossible*, Lyft's driver requirements make it highly unlikely: https://help.lyft.com/hc/en-us/articles/115012925687-Driver-requirements#dmv.

Good or bad, the quality of the experience is dictated by more than just the technology itself. If you don't actually have great people in place to service the customer (the employees, in our case), and if you lack the proper processes to create flow and link all the elements together, the technology won't serve you.

You also have to do things in the right order. Many organizations leap before they look by trying to put the technology in place first. Then they work backwards and say, "Now let's focus on the experience." But inevitably, they find that on Day 1, when people actually try to use these new systems, they're too hard to operate, or they don't make employees' lives any easier, or they're a bad fit with what's already in place.

The experience cannot be an afterthought. It must be the starting point and the guiding light for everything you do.

Lifting and Shifting: A Cautionary Tale

Like many other HR technologies, enterprise resource planning (ERP) has been re-molded by digital. Many firms are in the process of transitioning from an on-site ERP tool to cloud-based technology. But they often err in thinking that this upgrade alone is going to create a great user experience. That is lifting and shifting, not reimagining.

This is the fate that befell one twenty-five-thousand-person consulting firm that I worked with. They made the switch to a cloud-based ERP system, but it didn't catch on among the workforce. When the HR leaders who oversaw the transition queried employees, they were disappointed by the feedback they received: "This is essentially the same as what we were doing before, only the user interface looks a little bit better."

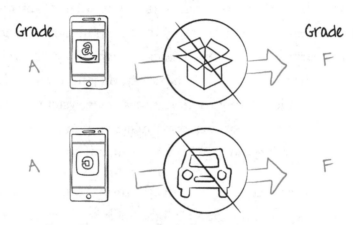

Illustration 13: Interface without an Experience

The company's first instinct was to blame the software. Technology is always an easy target because it doesn't have any feelings, and the vendor makes an easy target, too, because they're not part of the organization. It's not so easy to cast aspersions on the HR department when you have to work with them every day.

Blaming the vendor naturally leads to firing the vendor and replacing them with another software provider, as this consulting firm did. But because neither the software nor the vendor was actually the problem, nothing really changed.

Eventually, HR realized they had no one to blame but themselves. But the situation could easily have been avoided from the beginning had they put more thought into people and processes alongside the technology and tied all three elements—vision, strategy and mindset—together.

The whole ERP project was a costly mistake that took eighteen months and another five million dollars to rectify. In the end, the company essentially had to break down their ERP system and start over from scratch. Now they're doing much better, and they're well into the process of designing a workforce experience that any of their peers would envy. But sometimes you have to learn the hard way, even if it costs you time, effort, money, and, most importantly, credibility.

Moments that Matter

Consumers don't re-download a bad app, and employees don't forgive Phase 1 failures. You've really got only one chance to make a first impression, to move people, to convince them that you're reimagining the whole experience of working there and not just pushing out new technology for technology's sake—one chance to convey to them the real, day-to-day benefits of whatever new system you're trying to implement.

The most powerful way to achieve this is by building the workforce experience around what is called "moments that matter"—which happen to be one of the things I love about working in the HR field. Moments that matter are major life events and career milestones like getting hired, having a birthday, having a baby, earning a big promotion, getting married, etc. They represent an important intersection of the personal, the technological, and the professional, which makes them fertile ground for building and marketing a workforce experience program in a way that makes employees feel valued by the organization. Most don't know this, but as a former general manager at a major hotel chain in my younger years, these moments that matter were the things I enjoyed creating most, just as I do now. A room upgrade, flowers, room service credits—all bring on moments that matter.

How might you help create such moments? Well, say you're a manager and one of your employees has just given birth. In the whirlwind first days of motherhood, she's probably not thinking much about the job, but in the back of her mind she is aware of a host of issues to handle: maternity leave, adding the little one to the family health insurance plan, understanding the nuances of health coverage, company child care services, and so on. So many little things.

The last thing a frazzled new mother wants to do is comb through forty-five pages of health insurance fine print. The whole experience should be as frictionless as possible. That means you, as the manager, should be able to click one button on your team dashboard that efficiently triggers the "new parent" suite of services. Then the new mom gets a welcome email or text that says, "Congratulations on your new baby boy. Below are links to enroll your child in benefits. Here's information on maternity and paternity leave. And when you return to the office, there will be a few baby gifts waiting for you and your little one to enjoy."

Moments that matter are not necessarily just celebratory moments. HR needs to be there for employees in dark times, too. Marriage and parenthood mean changes to your income tax withholding and your insurance benefits, but the reverse sides of those coins are divorce and death, which also have tax and health insurance implications. And like the frazzled new mom, the last thing a recent divorcée or widow needs is hours of paperwork or time wasted on filling out redundant forms on a poorly designed website. Again, compassion demands that a frictionless experience be provided. After an appropriate amount of time has passed, an email could be sent that says something like, "We're so sorry to hear of the recent change in your family status. To help you keep your affairs as neatly ordered as possible at this difficult time, here are links to the pages you'll need to visit to change your health insurance details. Please let us know if there is anything else we can do for you."

Not only does this approach have obvious practical benefits for all parties, it also signals that the organization cares about its staff. Workforce technology functions best when it serves a human need. I'm really talking about a deeper emotional need here, beyond just, "Here's your paycheck." I'm referring to the need to feel valued and appreciated, part of something bigger than oneself, part of a community that cares.

Empathy is essential to the digital workforce experience. It's not just transactional ones and zeroes, cost benefit, and how much ROI we can squeeze out of a given piece of software. It's more "human," less "resources," if you will.

If a Training Program Is Rolled out in an Office, and No One's Around to Hear It, Did It Really Happen?

Organizations invest so many resources in recruiting. How do we attract the best talent? How do we retain the best talent? How do we grow our talent organically? An entire science has sprung up around the task of creating an organizational culture, promoting engagement, and cultivating loyalty.

We've spent forever trying to make people "feel good" at work, whether by setting up their cubes differently, giving them an office or open spaces in which to collaborate, taking away their open spaces to give them privacy, or by giving them kitchens with a spread of fresh muffins and OJ in the morning and a sushi platter every Thursday, or by putting healthy snacks in the vending machine, and so forth.

Employees like those perks, and they are indeed useful for developing a culture that people enjoy being part of (who doesn't want to step away from the desk and pop a handful of free California rolls or Combos?), but these measures can only go so far. They're still an analog solution for a digital world. We need another means of really reaching people where they are and giving them what they need.

Digital workforce technology is the intravenous (IV) solution that delivers those tools, helping to build the kind of organization where employees can be comfortable and work efficiently, without administrative roadblocks.

We could spend all of our time learning how to recruit better, how to train better, and how to get people more engaged, but without this experience platform in place, there is no way to get to our workers. The fluidity and flexibility of digital allow us to meet people where they are—in a literal as well as a figurative sense, since "where they are" is no longer necessarily in the next cube, or down the hall, or even in the same county.

The structure of white collar work has changed dramatically since the dawn of digital. The conventional model of everyone working in the same place, in the same office, at the same time has given way to flexible work arrangements and telecommuting. A 2016 Gallup poll found that 43 percent of Americans worked remotely at least part of the time.[2] And this trend is bound to expand as the information economy continues to reshape how and where we work.

2 "America's Coming Workplace: Home Alone," *Gallup*, March 15, 2017, http://news.gallup.com/businessjournal/206033/america-coming-workplace-home-alone.aspx.

Such changes decentralize the workplace experience. Our people are not sitting in the office reading posters on the wall; they are working at home, in coffee shops, and on airplanes. They're working during the day and at night, at irregular hours, all over the city, and maybe all over the planet. HR departments invest millions of dollars a year putting in place programs to keep and develop talent, but HR is not keeping up with the nature of work, and it's not rethinking how to deliver these programs.

Recall the definition of a frictionless digital workforce experience we introduced in chapter 1: delivering the right product to the right people at the right moment and through the right channel. Why spend millions on this stuff when there's not even a way to get it to those who need it?

Say you're the HR director of a large firm and you're rolling out an elaborate, expensive new training program for your workforce of several thousand people. But your staff is all over the map—both literally and figuratively: they have different kinds of jobs, their past experience varies, and they are geographically distributed from Los Angeles to London.

The digital workforce experience needs to be customized and personalized, made flexible and adaptable. If your training program isn't designed to accommodate each and every worker individually, based on their unique profiles and skill sets, and in a way that lets them engage with it fluidly, there's a problem.

How do you design such a program for such a multifaceted workforce? How do you even advertise it?

Traditionally, like most organizations, your HR department has promoted these programs by putting posters around the break room, publishing a blurb in the monthly office newsletter, and tacking some nice-looking signs above the urinals or inside the bathroom stalls. These days, you're a little more tech savvy, so you send a couple of mass emails to supplement the posters, but your company—like most organizations—is still trapped in analog thinking for a digital program.

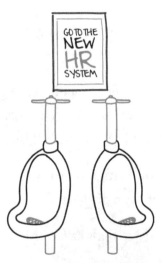

Illustration 14: "Potty Times"

We live in a world where some of our most important people may not even come into the office more than once a month. They may not be able to take part in the training. They may not even *know* about it. We can't expect them to make a special trip to HQ and visit the restroom just to stay apprised of training opportunities.

So you launch your learning program, but it soon becomes apparent that you're trying to apply a one-size-fits-all system to a diverse, decentralized workforce. Uh-oh. What now? You start sweating bullets during team meetings and taking more and more of your "coffee breaks" at the office beer fridge.

Given the cost of the initiative, the higher-ups are nervous about its ROI. Eventually, your boss calls you into his office and asks, "How's our new training program going?"

"Great! But it's not really getting to the people we need to reach."

"Well, if it's not getting to them, then I guess it's not 'great' at all, is it?" he says. (I've made this hypothetical boss a sarcastic jerk, for dramatic effect.) "Why the hell isn't it reaching them?"

"Uh, well, half of them don't work in the office anymore. And the other half of them did a similar training five years ago."

"How much did we budget for this thing? Give me the exact figure."

"A bazillion dollars."

Your boss explodes. "A bazillion! This is unacceptable! Get out of my office!" Then he bellows at his assistant, "Get Jason Averbook on the phone! He'll know how to handle this."

I make no immodest claims about my prowess as an HR problem solver, but I do know a thing or two about creating a digital workforce experience, and about why things go wrong. And it's clear in this example why it went awry.

Fortunately, I also know a few things about how to do it right. In the next few chapters, we'll take a closer look at some concrete steps you can take to create a great workforce experience in your own organization. We'll also examine the kind of thinking you need to develop the necessary vision, and detail the building blocks needed to execute it.

TAKEAWAYS

1. Workforce technology needs to be "consumerized."

Consider Lyft, Airbnb, Netflix, StubHub—all are disruptors that have become household names and have upended their respective industries and revolutionized consumers' expectations. This is the model for HR in the next five to ten years. Every company should strive for their workforce experience to be as strong as their consumer experience.

2. Look beyond the technology.

Whether at work or at play, the quality of an experience is determined by a lot more than just the technology itself (even if the interface looks slick). You need the right people and the right processes in place. You also need to utilize the right channel at the right time. All these elements synergize to produce the desired outcome. Technology alone can't carry the load.

3. Focus on moments that matter.

Moments that matter represent the crystallization of everything we in HR work for: the smooth integration of the personal, the professional, and the technological. Design your workforce experience around such moments. Employees should feel valued when they reach important milestones, and they should be able to instantly get the information they need at crucial times.

4. "Intravenous" delivery: send it straight to the heart.
Flexible, decentralized organizational structures mean your employees may be temporally and geographically dispersed. Digital technology provides the means by which we deliver the services and tools they need quickly, efficiently, and conveniently.

Mindset: Think Different

Hall of Fame baseball catcher Yogi Berra, who was known as much for his off-kilter witticisms as he was for his performance at the plate, famously said, "Ninety percent of the game is half mental." This is something I continually preach to my boys, Ben and Alex. Creating a digital workforce experience might not be an athletic competition, but Berra's aphorism still applies. Before your organization can *be* a certain way, you need to *have a certain mindset*—even if that means breaking with convention.

A Vision in Four Easy Steps

In previous chapters, we talked about the importance of a vision as the strategic plan underpinning everything you do. Every organization has a signature, a unique conception of the company and what it wants its workforce to be like. For example: "Support the organization's business strategy and people strategy by innovating new ways to deliver services and programs that meet the needs of our customers." That vision encapsulates in one sentence what the organization wants to be and how and to whom it will deliver value.

A well-constructed vision should possess four components. First, there's a *story*. Each organization has its own narrative—the tale it wants to tell about itself and its future. You should be able to deliver the story on a cocktail napkin in thirty seconds.

All great stories have one thing in common: the protagonist *wants* something—*desires* something—and must battle some antagonistic force to get it. Think of all the legendary tales and heroic epics that resonate with us emotionally and have provided inspiration for Hollywood for generations. The "hero's journey" is an enduring archetype because so much of life is an ongoing quest to overcome obstacles that stand in the way of what we desire. People respond and relate to that.

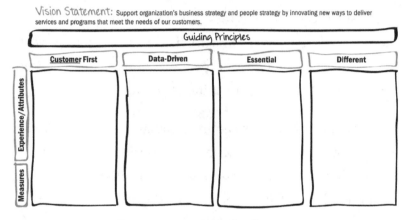

Vision Statement: Support organization's business strategy and people strategy by innovating new ways to deliver services and programs that meet the needs of our customers.

Illustration 15: Sample Client HR
Service Delivery Vision Map

The story behind your vision might not be expressed in terms of battles or quests or journeys, but there *will* be some underlying desire or purpose that moves the whole organization. What drives you? What is your mission?

Second, the vision should be supported by *guiding principles*. These are the values—such as data-driven, efficient, simple, global, transparent, easy, and flexible—that your workforce experience program seeks to uphold. They're guardrails that keep your program focused; without them, you'll veer off track.

For example, say one of your principles is "simple." Working at your company should be uncomplicated, fluid, hassle-free. If asking for time off means having three different supervisors sign off on a form, that is not simple. You must change your approach.

Or maybe being "accessible" is the prevailing value. Can employees access the tools they need anywhere, at any time? If they can only get into the system via the office intranet when they're at their desk between the hours of nine and five, well, you're not adhering to your principle of accessibility.

Attributes, which make up the third layer, are closely related to principles. Attributes describe the specific criteria needed to execute those principles. If one of your principles is being global, what does that look like? For starters, the interface needs to be in seven languages, it should be mobile-responsive/optimized and accessible anywhere, it must be GDPR compliant and supportive, and it should have a dedicated tech support team for when things go wrong.

In the example at the start of this section ("Support organization's business strategy and people strategy by innovating new ways to deliver services and programs that meet the needs of our customers"), one of the principles is "data-driven." Here are some corresponding attributes:

- Management has real-time access to role-based dashboards and reporting.

- I trust the data and can use it to identify patterns.

- I am confident using data to support both my decision-making and advice to others.

Measures constitute the fourth component of the vision, and they are important because they establish the standards by which you gauge your progress. How will we quantify whether we've succeeded (or failed)? How are we going to judge "simple"? How are we going to evaluate "global"? How are we going to measure "agile"? How do we determine if we're "fast"? For example, two measures that pair with the attribute of "data-driven" would be "data accuracy and usage (reports, dashboards)" and "improvement in HR analytical skills."

Measures are like a grizzled old boxing coach, firm but fair, ready to dole out praise when it's deserved or give it to us straight if we're faltering. They hold our feet to the fire and make sure we're living up to our principles and aspirations. Another key component of measures is that they oftentimes need to be translated into the language of who you are delivering the measure to. This concept of "storytelling" is important to bring into the overall program and vision.

It's a Team Effort

Obviously, the vision doesn't just materialize out of thin air. Someone has to sit down, put pen to paper, and string together the right words in the right order. When you get to the actual process of how to write it and whom to involve in that process, you should follow two guidelines: involve the executive stakeholders and be cross-functional in your approach.

Functional
Common Functional Expertise

System Analysts   Process Designers   Developers   Testers

Cross-functional
Representatives from the various functions

Sales, Finance, Operations

Illustration 16: Team Dynamics

As the leaders of the organization, the executives must be involved. They set the tone, they give the marching orders, and they take responsibility if things go off track. Executives are also in a special position to align the corporate strategy with the HR strategy. And because the vision has their blessing, the organization avoids a situation in which lower-level people are making decisions that will just get shot down by the executives later on. Moreover, executive stakeholders should be engaged not only in creating the vision, but also in executing it. It's not just a one-and-done, pass-the-torch situation. They're along for the whole ride.

However, although the execs spearhead the initiative, there's also a pluralistic element to creating a vision: it's not dreamed up by one or two of the top people and then handed down like an edict from on high. The vision planning team should be a cross-functional group of various organizational stakeholders. For example, if it's a retail company, the team should include not just the usual suspects (the C-suite, IT, HR, and perhaps accounting) but also people who work in the stores, local managers, regional managers, employees at the distribution centers—basically, a cross-section of everyone who is part of the workforce.

This is important because, again, you must consider your target market: if you want to design new tools and processes for a workforce experience, design them for the people who will be using them. It's like when corporations use focus groups to test products in development. They handpick participants who are diverse enough to provide a range of opinions, but who all fall within the product's target demographic.

The cross-functional approach is powerful because it gives everyone a seat at the table (literally, in some cases), but it also takes into account how the experience of using the same tools will play out differently in different contexts. An office worker who is in front of the computer all day will interface with an employee portal differently than, say, a delivery person who spends 90 percent of their shift on the road.

Two types of people should be recruited for the planning committee. First, there are those who already care about the workforce experience issue; maybe they've discussed it with you before. They're vocal about the need for changes, and they have a sense of what should be done.

You also want to involve people you haven't heard from before—those who aren't so vocal, but whose untapped opinions can provide useful insight into where they struggle with specific workforce issues and how their workday could be improved. Ask them questions to get a sense of how your ideas might work in practice: "Based on this prototype, would you use this? Does it make sense? Does it express what we've been thinking about in terms of vision? Will it make you feel better as an employee?" You may want to see if someone who has designed your customer experience should be involved as well.

As always, emphasize to the people who help you create the vision that *they* will benefit from it, so it isn't being done as a "favor" on top of the normal work they do. (And, of course, they should be duly compensated if there are extra hours involved.)

From a change management perspective, the people on the vision/planning committee will be an asset later, when it comes time to roll out the program. They will be your "change champions," helping to validate the vision among their peers by saying, "Guys, this isn't just another HR thing that they're forcing upon us. It was built with our input. And we know it'll make things better for all of us."

Earlier, we talked about how, eventually, after enough marketing from HR, the digital workforce experience becomes a natural part of the DNA. It's satisfying when you see that you no longer need to market it assiduously, because employees start marketing it to one another.

Basically, what we want to avoid is an insular, HR-centric approach. Looking at the workforce experience from every angle early in the process helps you anticipate how it will be received and how you'll need to communicate the change when the program is eventually launched.

Mindset Shift: Out with the Old (Fixed), in with the New (Growth)

Human beings are creatures of habit. We gravitate toward the familiar and we resist change. It's partly an evolutionary thing—our caveman brain predisposes us to be cautious of the unknown, an evolutionary vestige of a time when the unknown might have posed a lethal threat.

Nevertheless, even back in Paleolithic times, people knew they had to switch things up sometimes. One day, one caveman said to the other cavemen, "Guys, why are we always hunting in this part of the forest? I mean, it's nice and all, but why don't we ever cross the stream and go to the *other* part?"

To which his fellow cave people likely said, "The *other* part of the forest? Dude, no. Why would we do that? We've always done things this way."

After some pushing and prodding, the curious caveman eventually got his way. The little group expanded their domain. They ventured out; they hunted and gathered using new methods and in new territories—humanity's first workforce experience program!

Progress happens when people push past the comfort and stability of routine and force themselves to think differently. Before we get down to the details of designing processes and implementing technologies, we need to change our way of thinking by adapting a completely different mindset.

First, this means our conception of whom we're working for needs to evolve past an insular, HR-centric model to an outward-looking, consumerized one, with technologies and processes geared toward workers and managers who are not part of the HR department.

One of the things that we haven't done in human resources is put the employee at the center. We have been there to serve the employee, but have we thought about how we can serve them versus how they can have access to the information they need to make them successful in their roles? We've always put the HR department at the center. The answer to every employee problem or inquiry has been, "Just call us. We'll take care of it." If an employee had a concern, an elaborate sequence of manual HR heroics went on behind the scenes to address it. But because it was hidden from view—handled by HR people, within the cozy confines of our own department—the employee didn't know (nor did they care, necessarily) about the work that went into resolving their issue.

That worked for a while, sort of. But today, there are faster, easier, more efficient ways of doing things that are better for all stakeholders—HR, employees, managers, and the organization as a whole.

Now we're looking from the outside in, rather than the inside out. In every process we design, every policy we implement, every technology we use, we have to think differently in order to put the workforce at the center, to provide employees direct access to the digital workforce experience.

Shifting our mindset also means becoming more empathetic and figuring out how we can add value to the employees' experience, rather than primarily thinking about ourselves. Empathy allows us to better predict the challenges we may encounter along the way. For example, ordinarily, we might presume that employees will jump at the chance to use a new technology that should minimize time spent on weekly administrative tasks, but do we realize that those same employees have been bombarded with a half dozen other initiatives this month? Do we understand that they already have eight other tools they're expected to juggle? Can we appreciate the fact that a salesperson's main job is to meet their quota, or that a retail employee might not have access to a computer or even their own smartphone during most of the day, meaning that the tools we offer might not always be the godsend we expect them to be?

This kind of mindset shift goes hand in hand with "design thinking," which is a more innovative, solution-focused, action-oriented approach to creating. Design thinking puts people—the end users—at the center of planning and problem-solving. It's an effective approach for developing self-service tools that employees will use to do their jobs, but it also lets them play around with different functions, interact with the software, and—dare I say it—have a little fun with it.

As anyone who's ever tried to quit smoking, get on a steady exercise regimen, or argue with my uncle about politics on Thanksgiving can attest, changing one's mindset is difficult. And changing the thinking of a collective body (as opposed to an individual) is even harder. People tend cling to old processes for no other reason than because that's how they've been done for a while.

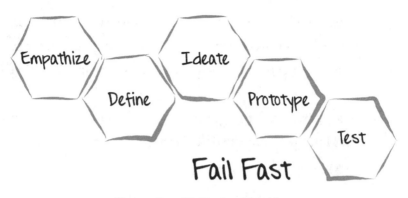

Illustration 17: Design Thinking

Even "enlightened" firms that understand the necessity of change often struggle because, simply, they don't put enough time into executing. If you don't make the time and marshal the resources to put your design into place, the results won't come. This is, once again, partly due to Shiny Object Syndrome, in the sense that organizations try to take the easy route by licensing a piece of technology without first doing the hard work of crafting and implementing a vision, changing their mindset, doing away with entrenched processes, etc. Remember, to create an excellent workforce experience, technology is only 10 percent of the formula. It is not a means for bypassing everything else.

Breaking and Rebuilding

Changing one's mindset means looking at things in a fundamentally new way—not just the old saw about thinking outside the box, but doing away with the box altogether. Take Einstein, for example. His achievements in physics were so groundbreaking because he didn't just add to existing theories; he developed an entirely new set of ideas (the general theory of relativity) that explained the physical universe in a way that Newtonian physics did not account for. (And if you think that analogy is a little too grandiose for the context, bear in mind that I'm known in the field as the "Einstein of workforce technology.")[1]

The purpose of thinking in a radically different way is learning how to *do* things in a radically different way, and that means the changes we are talking about are big, company-wide transformations, not small alterations. It's a major remodeling of the core, not tweaks around the margins. It's a process of breaking and rebuilding: we need to *break* from the status quo and *rebuild* something altogether different from what we had before.

Before embarking on such a monumental task, organizations will naturally want to ask, "How do I know whether I need to break and rebuild rather than just augment?" To answer that question, go back to your vision. Your organization may already be halfway there and may not need a major overhaul. But if there's a big gap between where you are today and where you want to be tomorrow, you'll need to break and rebuild.

Recently, while I was helping a large retail organization diagnose its workforce experience problems, I asked, "What

---

1 No one has ever called me the Einstein of workforce technology . . . yet.

does an employee in one of your stores do when they want to take time off? Walk me through the process, pretending that the employee is new and doesn't know anything."

So they opened up their portal, typed "I want to take time off" in the search bar, and got 261,000 hits. *Two hundred sixty-one thousand* documents dealing with taking leave.

"You've got to be kidding," I said. "Two hundred sixty-one thousand?"

"Well, that's not actually what the employee has to do," they said.

"Of course," I said. "I know that. But the *employee* doesn't!"

Something was wrong. And, as expected, the deeper we dug, the more it became clear that the company was in dire need of a break and rebuild; we needed to level the existing process and replace it with something newer, better—*different*.

Like shifting one's mindset, breaking and rebuilding clashes with human nature; people naturally resist change. We favor the path of least resistance and tend to apply Band-Aid solutions to problems that demand more extensive treatment.

And just as Einstein theorized a new physics rather than building on Newton's theory, you have to make a new process, not just add to the existing one. It's not enough to simply add tools to what you already have. That only makes things worse, because then you end up with two dozen different tools—an unnavigable jungle of techno-administrative "stuff."

Breaking and rebuilding is also a matter of governance, in terms of enforcing the new set of processes—drawing a hard line in the sand and saying, "This is where we stand now. Effective today, there's a new sheriff in town. That new sheriff is the vision. And she's a hard-ass when it comes to the law."

It means that everyone is going to work according to the vision, and it's going to be uncomfortable at first, because we've been doing things the same way for fifteen years. There are processes that Marcia put in place a decade ago that no longer apply. We all loved Marcia, but Marcia hasn't worked here since 2010.

In order to reinforce the new regime, HR has to break everyone of their old habits. HR also has to drop some old habits of its own—namely, doing things for employees that they are now capable of doing themselves.

For example, when an organization introduces a self-service module for employees and managers, it often takes time for them to learn how to use it. And if they can't figure it out, the first thing they do is reach for the phone and dial the HR help desk. Then, instead of teaching the employee how to use the technology (which is, of course, the very purpose of self-service), HR just handles it for them. But in the long run,

HR is doing them no favors: it just reinforces bad processes for everyone.

The old "Can you do it for me?" phone call is precisely the kind of opportunity we must avail ourselves of when we are marketing new technologies and processes and grinding old methods into the dust. If you want to make change happen, you must take away the familiar, easy option. You'll still be performing your duty to assist employees with their needs, but now you'll train them on the new processes in the technology. Give a man a fish, and you feed him for a day, but *teach* a man to fish, and he can enroll in direct deposit on his own.

Performance Mismanagement

One HR function that is crying out for a gut renovation is performance management. Many managers express deep dissatisfaction with the performance management process, which in most firms means the annual burden of filling out a report and assigning some sort of rating to each of their employees based on how they've done over the past twelve months.

Thinking that managers don't like the tedium of so much paperwork, people in some organizations have said, "Let's update our performance management process. They hate filling out the forms, so let's digitize it instead."

However, the folks in these firms have misdiagnosed the problem, because what managers resent is not the paper-pushing;

it's the *process*. These managers say, "Look, I can't really remember how every single employee performed during the whole year, and this is a once-a-year task. I barely remember what they did in the last two weeks."

Taking a bad process and putting it online doesn't help. It might look slick, it might be mobile-friendly, but fundamentally, it's unchanged.

We need to break that antiquated approach and rebuild it. Instead of squeezing in performance reviews once at the end of the fiscal year, let's provide routine feedback during the whole twelve months. Managers will now have the ability to keep better track of how their people are performing, and employees will enjoy the benefit of continuous feedback and coaching, which many workers (particularly younger ones) thrive on.

Employee portals also present fertile ground for a break and rebuild. I've helped many organizations reimagine their portals, which usually operate more or less in the following fashion: say you've just had a baby. You open up the portal, search around for the Human Resources link somewhere at the bottom, then venture into the messy HR page in search of another link that says "Benefits." Then you find the button that says, "I just had a baby," and click on Beneficiaries. At *best*, it's tedious and time-consuming; at worst, you can't find what you're looking for.

Instead, what if we personalize each employee's portal? What are the ten things Ron in sales does most frequently?

Now, when Ron opens up the portal, the things he needs are front and center, and he doesn't have to navigate a labyrinth of links.

That's an example of not merely putting in a new technology, but doing away with an old paradigm altogether by saying, "Instead of making people navigate the portal, let's customize it based on their habits and bring the tools they need right to the front."

One of the great advantages of this new paradigm, something we'll go into more later in the book, is that the jump in productivity and efficiency achieved by breaking and rebuilding opens up new avenues for HR staff to focus on what they're best at. One of our objectives is to reduce our paper-pushing workload so we can devote more time to sensitive issues that technology can't handle—things like, "I was sexually harassed by a colleague," or, "I've had a death in my family," or, "I'm trying to get promoted and my boss is telling me I can't be."

Let humans handle what humans excel at (empathy, emotional intelligence, social nuance, language—basically, dealing with other humans), and let machines handle what machines excel at. Generally, that means tasks that are "RAD": repeatable, auditable, and documented. If it's a repeatable task I can easily audit and document, it's very likely a computer will do a better job of it than I will. We no longer need to pay people $100,000 a year to manually fat-finger data into a database, or to fax a form, or to register an employee's change of address.

Most industries are in a kind of in-between, awkward adolescent phase when it comes to adjusting to the sweep of digital technology. On the one hand, those of us who have been in the business for a while have lived long enough to witness the shift from the mainframe era to dial-up to what we have today, and we've grown accustomed to those changes.

On the other hand, a new wave of even more radical technologies (AI, bots) is looming. The notion of "computers doing humans' work" is both exhilarating and strange, and it is understandable that HR professionals might have mixed feelings about it.

As Yogi Berra once said, "The future ain't what it used to be." We may not have anticipated the impact of digital technology on our profession when we were younger. We may not have even seen it coming ten years ago. But now that it's here, let's embrace it with enthusiasm. Our time is now!

TAKEAWAYS

1. A vision comprises four main elements: story, principles, attributes, and measures.

The story relates to your organization's mission: what goal are you pursuing as an organization? Principles are the values that define you. Attributes are the criteria that make up those principles. And measures are the means by which you evaluate your progress.

2. Change the mindset.

Instead of thinking of HR as being at the center, place the worker at the center. Empathize with employees' needs, problems, and desires. Pursue a paradigm of "consumerization" of HR to get up to speed with the technological innovations that have changed how people shop, play, live, and work.

3. Break and rebuild.

It's not enough to just add new tools to your existing process, make minor tweaks, or adjust a process or two. If what you have today doesn't closely resemble what you've articulated in your vision, you'll need to break with the existing model and rebuild it from the foundation up.

A Foundation of Data:
Business is Personal(ized)

I'm sure we've all had this experience at one time or another: you're idly clicking around Amazon when a product pops up in the "Recommended for You" list that just happens to be *exactly* what you wanted—and you didn't even know you wanted it! Maybe you didn't even know it existed.

Or you're combing through the Netflix catalogue when the "Top Picks for You" algorithm comes up with some obscure foreign movie that suits your particular taste profile so well, it's almost as if the film had been made for you.

These hyper-personalized recommendations sometimes feel uncanny in their accuracy, as if Amazon and Netflix know us better than we know ourselves. They are possible because of the brilliant ways those companies handle data—endless terabytes of it, collected from millions of users round the clock. What these companies and many others have done with data has revolutionized the online consumer experience, turning the world into everyone's personal shopping mall and movie theater.

Now these data techniques are spilling into the workplace, allowing human resources departments to provide the same kind of laser-focused personalization for employees. Data is really the foundation of the whole workforce experience. That means having strong processes in place to get it, keep it current, and make sure that it's used in the right way.

Data-driven personalization offers a number of exciting new applications. It can be used for something as simple

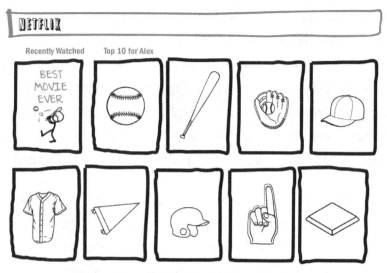

Illustration 18: Netflix—Personalization

as automatically sending out a "Happy Birthday" note or a message celebrating an employee's one-year anniversary with the firm—little gestures that make people feel appreciated and loved. If you have kids, it could deliver notifications about special company perks and benefits for parents. Or, if the forecast is calling for snow that morning, the system might send an alert to your smartphone that says, "Heavy snow is predicted today. Would you like to work from home?"

In addition, a personalized workforce experience can zero in on each employee's talents and ambitions by delivering training and career development programs based on their data profile. For example, if an employee has expressed interest in becoming a general manager (because, say, they ticked off a box on a form somewhere or signed up for a certain newsletter), the system will deliver messages about leadership and management classes. Or, if an employee has stated a desire to learn Spanish (maybe because she wrote down "Spanish—beginner" on her resume when she first applied), the system will notify her of company-sponsored language courses. This is the embodiment of something we talked about in chapter 1—delivering the right service to the right people at the right moment through the right channel.

Having good data is also invaluable in fielding common HR-related questions, such as, "How many vacation days do I have left?" If your data foundation is strong, an employee should be able to retrieve that information with one click on the portal landing page, or even better, by asking, "Siri, what's my vacation balance?" That's certainly preferable to querying the manager, who has to check with HR, who then might take a day or two to respond—all to answer a simple question that should be answerable within fifteen seconds.

It's simple, really: the better the data you have—in both quantity and quality—the better the workforce experience will be. The more granular the data is, the more nuanced and sophisticated will be your understanding of each person's wants, needs, likes, and dislikes. With good data, you'll be better positioned to personalize your communication, fine-tune your message, and fully leverage the assets of your workforce.

One of the questions I always ask clients is, "Who knows more about your workforce? You as a company or LinkedIn?"

Most organizations stay up to date on only the basic information (name, address, department, start date), while the average LinkedIn profile is a veritable trove of employee data—location, work history, accomplishments, professional connections, skills, endorsements, and interests. There's no reason we shouldn't have the same information at our fingertips. (And, by the way, if LinkedIn knows more about your people than you do, so do your competitors!)

Cracks in the Foundation: What to Avoid

New technologies like Siri and Alexa offer exciting avenues for enhancing the workforce experience, but you can't paper over data deficiencies just by acquiring slick gadgets or fancy software. That's like putting frosting on a moldy cake. It might look pretty and even taste good for a half second, but the moment your taste buds react to the rot under the surface, you'll spit it back out. Good data is the foundation.

The first thing to remember is that each organization is a unique entity, with its own workforce characteristics, and its foundation must be designed with those particulars in mind. Last year, I was hired by a healthcare organization that has three dozen locations employing full-time employees, part-time employees, contractors, H-1B visa holders, temp workers, and veterans who'd been there for decades—everyone from MRI machine technicians to gift shop clerks to hospital administrators to gastroenterologists. They all have different work-related wants and needs, and they all interface with technology differently. For a gift shop clerk, the most useful workforce experience device might be the point-of-sale system. For a doctor, it will probably be their smartphone or a desktop PC sitting in the emergency room somewhere. For an administrator, it'll be the computer on their desk. Other personnel might use a shared iPad. The point is that you have to design the right channel for the right people in the right setting. Then you have to communicate to all those people that they need to use the tools properly and follow processes correctly to keep the data current. The personalized workforce experience is only as good as the information we feed into it.

Needless to say, it is a challenge to custom-design a data system for such a vast, multifaceted organization and then get the workforce on board with maintaining good data. But if it's done right, that foundation can serve you for years to come.

Often, those in organizations have only a dim sense of how their data processes work or how they could be improved. They're not used to thinking about data as having utility beyond the most obvious applications: that it's not just something that sits in a box somewhere, but is something that forms a dynamic, breathing part of the organization. Like all disruptive ideas, this takes some getting used to.

One way I like to diagnose an organization's data architecture is by "following the yellow brick road" of an employee's information, from job application to onboarding to employment to retirement.

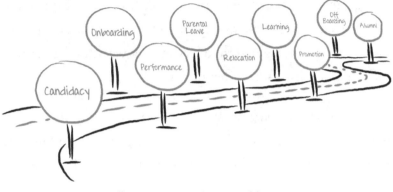

Illustration 19: Journey Maps

When a candidate submits an application, where does all that information go? Usually, it just sits somewhere, even after the person is hired. Then they spend their first day on the job filling out another round of paperwork, most of which duplicates what they already submitted on their application. With each passing year, as they get promoted, or they transfer, or they learn new skills, more data accumulates, only to be relegated to some far-flung corner (digital or otherwise) of the company's record-keeping system—*if* the information is preserved at all.

Ideally, all that data should follow the employee from one phase to the next, without anyone having to manually input it each time. What happens instead in most organizations is what I call "data leakage": It gets lost because information is keyed in wrongly when someone misspells a name or records a date of birth by DDMMYYYY instead of MMDDYYYY. Or it's not keyed in at all because one department doesn't need it, even though another department does (or will, years later). Recruiting, training, employee relations— they all have their own data entry processes and storage methods. And so a wealth of untapped information just sits in different desert islands, left to decay.

This is another symptom of operating in silos, and it shows why siloed thinking is detrimental to the goal of seamlessness. Digital empathy is the best way to break silos within the HR function.

To dive deeper into the practical applications of good data, and to understand what opportunities we might miss out on, consider the following hypothetical example: you remember Manny, from chapter 1. When he first applied, the company got his profile in his application: where he went to school, where he used to work, titles and certifications, awards, aspirations, all of that stuff. That's rich, robust, useful data.

But as soon as Manny was hired, the firm filtered out most of that application data and retained only the bare minimum necessary for him to get his paycheck: name, address, department, and salary. Everything else was lost. That leakage is as harmful to a thriving workforce experience as an oxygen tank leak is to a pleasant scuba dive. You immediately have lost a ton of data that can be used to drive content and context to your workforce, a key experience mandate.

Fast-forward a year or two. Manny has been doing well in his position and is starting to consider his long-term role there. He's thinking about career development options, but he doesn't even know where to start.

Meanwhile, his manager, appreciating Manny's ambition (and the fact that he doesn't use annoying words like *vacay* or *hump day*), thinks, "I'd love to be able to enroll him in some extra training. Help him reach his career goals. It would be good for him *and* the firm."

But what *are* Manny's career goals, the manager wonders? "Well, um . . . he's an accountant, so I guess he's interested in . . . accounting." Well, that's not good data, it's just a self-evident fact. You can glean it from Manny's business card. "Uh, I know he likes hip-hop. And seafood."

Unless you are fortunate enough to work for an organization that organizes "Hip-Hop and Seafood Career Development" seminars, you're going to need better data if you really want to direct the right learning opportunities to the right people. What's more, who is good at what should not be a big mystery: Manny and everyone else already submitted this information when they applied, but it leaked from the system long ago.

Now, you could say, "Well, if Manny wants to undergo training, or his boss wants to involve his team in certain opportunities, why don't they just ask? Do they really need computers to tell them what to do?"

There is some merit to this argument. Nothing is preventing them from "just asking." However, even the best-informed managers don't know everything about everything. And employees are even more in the dark when it comes to the learning and development avenues available to them.

Our goal is to create a frictionless experience wherein people don't *have* to ask, don't have to go out of their way to find information—the resources they need are delivered to them automatically, with the same smooth efficiency of Amazon and its propensity for conveniently recommending exactly what you need, when you need it.

A question I often ask of organizations when I evaluate the strength of their data processes is, "How many times is an employee's name entered by HR?" If the answer is more than zero, you have a data problem. Ideally, an employee should put down their name once when they fill out the job application, and then it should never be entered again. It should flow seamlessly along between departments until that employee leaves the company.

The responsibility for keeping good data falls primarily, but not *exclusively*, on the human resources department. Much like the responsibility to care for the earth is shared by everyone, keeping data clean and robust is a collective, organization-wide job.

That means emphasizing the fact that the employees own their own data. It means following the established processes for gathering, updating, and storing data. It means having effective governance mechanisms in place, and enforcing the rules as needed to make sure each person is doing what they're supposed to be doing.

We have to be sensitive about how we sell this last point. People balk if they feel they're being asked to do someone else's job. We're paying our workforce to sell vitamins in a retail store or to keep patients healthy or to serve coffee. We're not paying them to keep their data clean and current. It needs to be woven into our messaging that in order to create a great workforce experience, it's imperative to have a good, solid, clean foundation. It's dependent on all of us as an organization to do that—and by doing so, we all reap the rewards.

TAKEAWAYS

1. The better the data you have, the higher the level of personalization you can deliver.

Together, members of an organization make up a collective body, but each person has a unique set of interests, goals, and skills. More than at any other time in human history, digital and mobile technologies allow us to customize, personalize, and individualize the workforce experience for each person in a way that lets us fully leverage their skills and accommodate their interests.

2. How many times are you entering a person's name?

It better be zero! Once a job applicant enters their information into the system, it should follow them along fluidly, from department to department, year to year, staying clean, cohesive, and up to date. This is crucial to your experience architecture.

3. The foundation stays strong if everyone does their part.

Governance is key. The HR department oversees the task of maintaining a robust foundation of data, but it's a collective effort. Enforcement of rules is helpful, but the best way to win buy-in is through softer means: emphasize the "what's in it for me?" angle, and people will do what is asked of them.

7

The Building Blocks of the Workforce Experience

Thus far, we've established the main concepts that underpin a workforce experience, and we've set up the foundation on which to build it: good data. Now, on top of that foundation, we can start stacking the building blocks of the program: high-touch service, user feedback, and a dedication to continuous improvement.

Illustration 20: High-Touch Service

Donning the Digital White Gloves

Managing humans and managing machines are two very different things. If a machine is broken, you call a technician, who tinkers with its components until it's fixed, and the machine is good to go for another couple of years.

Humans are more complex. When it comes to managing a multigenerational, multicultural workforce, every single day obstacles will arise. Someone wakes up in a bad mood, someone sexually harasses a colleague, someone has a death in the family, someone's kid gets sick. It's endless.

Human resources departments have been managing through these challenges for a while—at least since the advent of modern HR management during the industrial era. The profession was very different then, but human nature is largely unchanged.

A lot has changed culturally, economically, and technologically since the nineteenth century, but the challenge of figuring out how to serve people remains. HR has always struggled with balancing the strategic/corporate stuff with the interpersonal/transactional stuff. That's something every HR department needs to do to determine in its vision: what kind of service do we want to provide? And how do we provide it?

Traditionally, the phrase *white-glove service* has been synonymous with providing meticulous care and attention to a customer's every need. Service par excellence, the crème de la crème, the concierge treatment—service so nice that you've got to use French words to describe it.

In HR and other fields, the white-glove treatment goes by another name: "high touch." Am I supposed to be talking about "touching" and "HR" in the same sentence? Until recently, the ideal of HR service consisted of having well-trained professionals handle individual employee issues with a high level of personal interaction. But in recent years, this has been called into question. It's not that people don't want excellent service—obviously they do. It just means that they don't necessarily want or need that human touch, giving rise to a new paradigm, what I call "high-touch digital."

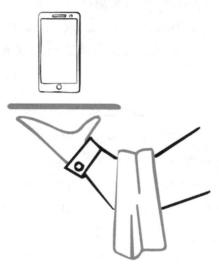

Illustration 21: High-Touch Digital

High-touch digital might seem at first glance like an oxymoron, but it just means taking advantage of the technology we now enjoy to deliver quality service without depending on human labor. We're seeing this more and more in the consumer world, as well as in the workforce. If people need to answer a question or complete a task, they prefer the shortest, simplest, easiest, most efficient method, which usually means avoiding telephone calls or face-to-face interaction.

It might take the form of interacting with a chatbot instead of visiting the help desk. It might be typing a question into a search bar and getting the desired information instantly, instead of spending five minutes listening to the customer service hotline's "please hold" music. It might mean ordering a product—whether it's a bundle of office supplies for work or a burger at a fast-food restaurant—on a touch screen or mobile app rather than with a person.

High-touch digital can be applied to more complex tasks, too. Let's say you're a manager and you want to give one of your top employees a raise. The high-touch human approach would be to call up someone in HR and say, "So-and-so has really performed well this year. She's an asset to the team, and I'd like to increase her salary." Then the HR person would explain the protocol and maybe ask some follow-up questions about so-and-so's performance.

A high-touch digital solution, on the other hand, would be typing "how to give someone a raise" into the portal (personalized to the manager) and reading about the procedure online. The tool could also ask questions about performance, perhaps having the manager assess the employee's work as "excellent," "very good," or "good," or assigning the quality a numerical rating from one to ten.

Then, the tool could automatically suggest a certain raise based on the employee's pay grade and the manager's rating: a 5-percent increase for "excellent," 4 percent for "very good," and so forth. If you are not using ratings, the experience could remind you to do a check-in and actually have a conversation with the worker (a much better method than ratings).

In essence, it's the same attentive, walk-me-through-my-options service that you'd get from a human, but it's systematized, and ultimately more efficient.

It's not that high-touch human service is obsolete, just that it's not the only game in town anymore. Almost all companies designing a workforce experience will pursue a kind of hybrid strategy, selectively employing both high-touch human and high-touch digital, thanks to the natural division of labor we discussed in chapter 5. Humans are better suited for certain tasks, and machines are engineered for other ones. The fundamental question all organizations must ask themselves is, "Do we want our vision to be primarily high-touch human or high-touch digital?"

Whichever path you take, you have to think about the needs of your customers—outside-in, workforce-centric rather than inside-out, HR-centric. And that means understanding who they are. Today, there might be four "generations" working under the same roof, usually with a wide range of preferences about how they want to get things done. Digital natives (born or brought up during the age of digital technology) tend to gravitate toward digital solutions. Digital immigrants (born or brought up before the widespread use of digital technology) might still feel more comfortable on the phone or handling things face to face.

Your vision needs to accommodate all groups if you want people to feel good at work. That means you must consider not just the demographics of the workforce, but its "technographics": how tech-savvy are they? How open are they to learning new tools and processes? If you're serving a hospital full of surgeons who have been doing appendectomies for twenty years, they're probably not going to want to spend time looking online for tools to do things. If you're working with executives who still have their assistant print out their emails for them, they might not care one bit if the portal is mobile-friendly. If your office is staffed by twenty-five-year-olds who don't know what an answering machine is, then it's a different picture altogether.

Just choosing where to apply a high-touch digital strategy versus a high-touch human approach is only half the battle. It doesn't mean anything if you don't secure buy-in from the people who will actually be using these services. I recall one situation in which HR launched a few digital service technologies intended to take humans out of the picture, but the organization had developed its vision with little input from the lower levels of the firm. Unsurprisingly, when the new system was launched, the workers were less than thrilled.

HR tried hard to market the new system and teach people how to use it, but failed to win the cooperation of managers, who simply told their subordinates, "You want to request leave or change your address? Don't bother with HR's online nonsense. We'll take care of it for you."

If managers are circumventing the system and handling everything themselves, the whole digital workforce experience remains underutilized. You also miss out on the valuable collection of data on which the experience is based.

The bottom line is that as you develop your service strategy, you must keep in mind what your workforce wants, not what you think they want. Understand your target demographic: that's a principle of marketing so fundamental that even we HR folks can understand it!

The Value of Feedback

A digital workforce experience is not a one-way street. It's not just HR or corporate unrolling new initiatives, imposing new processes, and pushing out changes in a unidirectional fashion. The line of communication also flows from the workforce back to HR in the form of rich, robust feedback that allows us to tinker with and tweak the program and quickly resolve technical issues. Feedback also enables us to amplify the degree of personalization and elevate the experience in a way that would have been impossible only a few years ago, before digital technology (and data analytics, in particular) so sweepingly changed the way we live.

Organizations work very hard to design a workforce experience around day-to-day transactions and moments that matter. But without measuring how employees *feel* when engaging with the tools we're creating, it's difficult to assess our progress.

Maybe once a year HR departments send out surveys composed of broad questions like, "How do you feel about working here?" or, "What can we do differently to improve the culture?" Such surveys are helpful, but inadequate (and also tend to generate a low response rate). They don't capture the precise "micro feedback" in real time (or almost real time) about the myriad processes, transactions, and interactions employees undertake daily and weekly.

This is another area in which we should emulate the practices of the consumer industry, which solicits mountains of instantaneous data from customers on browsing, purchasing, and every other phase of the digital shopping experience. Companies mine this information to produce a detailed portrait of what consumers want, when they want it, and how they want to buy it.

We should strive for that level of granularity and immediacy, so we can know how employees feel at work (especially during moments that matter) in real time, not a year later.

One big advantage of doing things this way is that up-to-date feedback about a specific process or tool lets us rectify problems quickly. We don't have to wait until the end of the year when HR is sending its third e-mail begging everyone to "please submit your annual employee satisfaction survey" before the whole office decamps for the holiday break. An always-on feedback loop lets us fix errors with strike-force rapidity and surgical precision.

However, with everyone piling in on the big data arms race, there is a risk of feedback fatigue if consumers feel bombarded with requests to fill out surveys, give ratings, and answer questions. To avoid this, keep your feedback format very simple: a smile sheet, a yes or no question like "Did this help you?" or maybe a single, quick five-star rating. No multi-question surveys or open-ended commentary. When it comes to transactional feedback, we just want to know about their general sentiment in that precise moment. A little bit goes a long way.

Go Live and Stay Live: Always Be Improving

Next time you're hankering for a dose of nostalgia, take a look at screenshots of popular websites from twenty years ago—Yahoo.com, for example, or the old *New York Times* home page. They look downright primitive without the rich functionality and aesthetic adornments we're used to seeing today.

We can laugh at the rudimentary state of the early web and remember the days when a few low-res JPGs and some HTML code looked so state of the art. But there's an important lesson in there, too: to keep people engaged, you have to be constantly growing, changing, and expanding. Even pages or portals that are only one or two years old start feeling stale if they don't give users new designs to look at and new features to play with.

Your organization's digital workforce experience should undergo a process of continuous improvement, with a team

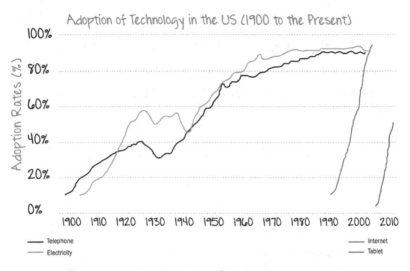

Illustration 22: Adoption of Technology in the US

dedicated specifically to making sure it happens. Changes shouldn't just occur once in a blue moon. Strive to unveil something new around every nine weeks, whether it's a tool, a function, a service, or even just a design alteration.

After all the planning and preparation you invest in building a workforce experience, going live is not the end; it's really just the beginning, if you're approaching it with that perpetual beta philosophy. The program (and it *is* a program, not a project) doesn't just sit there, static, after the debut. It's a living organism that you need to nurture so that it thrives.

Continuous improvement also goes hand in hand with collecting user feedback, which provides a steady stream of information about which aspects of the workforce experience are functioning and which are not. Most organizations are not accustomed to moving quickly when something in the process breaks. They're still operating under a mindset where fixing problems requires testing, requesting funding, and assembling a new team to resolve it. That kind of approach doesn't work anymore.

Another important component of "continuous improvement" is what I like to call "keeping up with the rest of the world." When all of a sudden the iPhone X shakes up the smartphone market, and now facial recognition is the hot new way to sign in, you better start thinking about whether and how that technology could improve the experience in your company.

Don't make keeping up with the world more complicated than it needs to be. Just keep close track of the consumer technology market: what it's doing, where it's headed, how tastes are changing, what consumers want. That provides you an abundance of ideas about how to upgrade the experience for your employees.

Analytics:
Deepen Your Intelligence Gathering

Analytics and intelligence are things organizations struggle with, but they're closely tied to data, feedback, and measuring what matters. One important aspect of analytics is establishing service-level agreements. That means asking yourself, in essence, "From a servicing standpoint, what do I promise the workforce? And how do I put that out there so that I can be held accountable for it?" They're benchmarks for quality control that hold you to a certain standard and keep you true to your vision. For example, a service-level agreement might be: "If employees call a service center, someone will always get back to them within four hours," or, "If someone submits a case online, an agent will respond within an hour." It can even be as simple as, "Our online chat system will be staffed eighteen hours a day."

By measuring how well you're complying with service-level agreements, you can quantify your progress toward fulfilling the vision and delivering good service.

A big advantage of analytics is that it lets you concretely demonstrate the value you're adding to the organization. *Workforce experience, moments that matter,* and *how employees feel* are somewhat abstract concepts. It can be challenging to accurately gauge the impact the HR function is having on people when there are so many other factors that influence how they feel at work—including factors that have nothing to do with their job at all. If you can point to clear evidence of the impact of new processes and technologies (e.g., 93 percent of service calls received a response within two hours, or 77 percent of new employees reported feeling satisfied with the onboarding procedure), it helps validate your effort.

TAKEAWAYS

1. **From high touch to high tech**

Providing white-glove service is a tall order. Thankfully, innovative processes and digital and mobile technologies let us serve more people with less human labor. High-touch digital can coexist with and complement high-touch human service within an organization. Different approaches are suited to different functions (and different types of workers, depending on their "technographic" profile).

2. **Some things never change.**

Even with the steady advance of AI, humans are better at handling emotionally sensitive and situation-specific problems. Machines are better at RAD (repeated, auditable, and documented tasks). Letting technology do more of the RAD heavy lifting gives HR professionals more time to handle more complex, "human" issues.

3. **Feedback: identify strengths and target weaknesses now, not later.**

Micro feedback tells us how employees are interacting with technology when they're interacting with it, rather than asking them to recall things that happened months ago. This permits focused, continuous improvement.

8

How to Get There:
From Strategy to Deployment

Planning a strategy essentially means coming up with a list of directions that guide you from point A (where you are now) to point B (where you want to end up). It sounds simple, but the line that connects those two endpoints is not straight. It twists and turns as you make all kinds of stops along the way. Those in-between stops represent the myriad tasks you must complete to execute the strategy.

Whether you operate a small firm of ten employees or head the HR department of a massive conglomerate, creating a workforce experience program is always a complex undertaking involving numerous moving parts. You have to deal with an array of projects—and projects within projects. You have to implement a handful of different technologies and redesign processes so everything fits together smoothly. And, of course, you need to ensure the coordination of multiple departments and stake-holders—many of whom have probably never worked together on anything, much less an organization-wide program like this one.

All in all, there's a lot of "stuff" going on at any one time in the process of creating a workforce experience strategy. Effective strategizing comes down to figuring out how to prioritize all those different tasks.

Prioritization isn't merely doing the most important things first; it's doing *the right things in the right order*. Often, you'll find that major components of the program are deferred until later in the process because they're contingent upon the completion of other, smaller tasks earlier in the timeline. Those earlier things might be very simple, even seemingly insignificant, but they pave the way for more significant elements down the line.

An urgency-impact matrix is a valuable tool for figuring out what needs to be done and when. You can visualize where tasks fall along the two axes (urgency and impact), which range from "low" to "high." Obviously, high-impact, high-urgency tasks should be dealt with expediently. Low-impact, low-urgency problems are generally placed toward the bottom of the to-do list. Tasks whose impact-urgency profiles are mixed (high-impact, low-urgency, or low-impact, high-urgency) warrant attention, but perhaps not immediately. You must weigh their prioritization in the context of everything else you have to do.

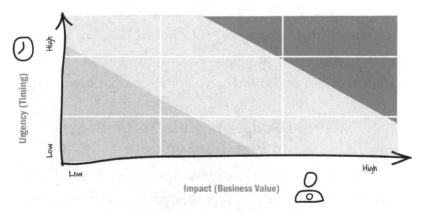

Illustration 23: Urgency-Impact Matrix

Building and executing a long-term strategy also means that there may be few visible signs of your progress as you piece together the underlying structure of the workforce experience. It takes a lot of work and a lot of waiting before you can taste the fruits of your labor. For example, since data is your foundation, you might spend six months building the organization's data architecture from the ground up. Most of the workforce won't feel the impact for a long time, since this behind-the-scenes work doesn't generate tangible results until it's been up and running for a while.

We have to think long-term; when it comes to strategy and planning, there is no instant gratification—the reward comes months or years down the line. It's not unlike constructing a house: it takes a long time for the motley pile of concrete, timber, and plumbing fixtures to begin to resemble a livable abode, and longer still before you can move in. But the moment you cross the threshold and look around, knowing that it's all yours, it becomes a home. Your home. We want to inspire similar feelings in our employees: a feeling of ownership, of belonging, and of comfort, even if the wait has been long.

Mindset/People/Process/Technology: In Sync, but Separate

With few exceptions, each task in your plan will be divisible into four elements: mindset, people, process, and technology. These components are distinct, but cohesive; separable, but constituting a whole.

Organizations stumble when they try to oversimplify things by lumping together mindset, people, process, and technology.

For example, if one of your many to-do items is "Develop a new onboarding protocol," that's an unhelpful oversimplification. The phrasing indicates *what* needs to be done, but it doesn't say anything concrete about *how* it is to be done. It is akin to teaching someone how to change the oil in their car by saying, "Step 1: Remove filter. Step 2: Change oil." OK, thanks but . . . how do I change the oil? Some people can't even find the filter on their coffee maker.

Instead of saying, "Develop a new onboarding protocol," you have to break that task down by specifying what needs to be done: "To create a new onboarding protocol, which people do we need? What processes must we design and implement? What technologies are necessary?"

Let's say that one of your tasks is digitizing performance reviews, which we discussed in the last chapter. In terms of people, you would need to secure the cooperation of managers and make sure they're willing and able to conduct performance reviews more frequently. The process part of the equation is a question of frequency: instead of making performance evaluations a once-a-year affair, now they will be monthly. Finally, with respect to the technology, we have to develop an interface that can accommodate the new protocol and make sure it's integrated with the data architecture of the system as a whole.

Breaking each step into a tripartite list of needs makes achieving that step simple and manageable.

One common pitfall we've discussed often throughout the book is overemphasizing the technological component, or thinking of the digital workforce experience as primarily a tech-driven initiative. The technology is obviously an essential part, but don't think of it as the center of the workforce solar system, around which the other two components orbit. Remember the formula: 20 percent mindset, 25 percent people, 45 percent process, 10 percent technology.

It is important to clarify that when we talk about dividing things into mindset, people, process, and technology, we're talking about the *tasks* (or "action items"). This does not mean that there should be four different *strategies* independent of one another. Organizations sometimes err by creating one strategy for "process," one strategy for "people," and one strategy for "technology," completely forgetting mindset and then struggling awkwardly to harmonize them. It just won't work. These organizations inevitably find that the technology may be in place, but the people and process components aren't ready yet, or the technology and processes are in sync, but the right people have not been mobilized.

This is also why it's crucial to maintain that cross-functional element throughout the process of strategy development to ensure that all the different departments, working groups, committees, and so on, are synergized.

If things go awry during strategy planning, it usually happens like this: the workforce experience team comes up with a plan, shows it to a few people in their orbit, and secures the necessary funding. Then, after working on the project for nine months, just as they're getting ready to roll it out to the whole organization, they realize they've neglected something important. "Hmm, maybe we should let the retail managers know what we're doing. And we should probably get marketing to develop some kind of branding or promotional materials for this project."

Of course, the retail managers have their hands full with their own projects, and the marketing people complain that there's no way they can put together a major campaign in such a short time. Suddenly, the project you thought was ready to launch two weeks from now has to be postponed as you scramble to get on board all the people you should have been coordinating with months ago.

Everyone involved in the workforce experience program has to sign off on the strategy from the beginning, know their role, and understand how that role intersects with the roles of other actors. It is indeed a major undertaking, but a little bit of effort in the early stages saves a lot of headache down the line.

Countdown to Launch: Deployment

People tend to think of deployment as a singular event, like pressing a big, red LAUNCH button and watching with a satisfied smile as the workforce experience machine rattles to life. Deployment, however, is more a process than a moment—a bunch of things happening over time rather than one thing happening once.

To fully understand the nature of deployment, we should also be clear on the terminology we use. The terms *deployment* and *implementation* are often used interchangeably, but they're not synonymous. Deployment is broader in nature. Like the digital workforce experience itself, deployment is more a program than a project—something that happens over the long term rather than just a one-and-done "go live."

Implementation, in contrast, is less strategic than tactical. The word describes the more practical or concrete aspects of putting things together—i.e., you would *implement* a piece of technology, but you would *deploy* a workforce experience. Training people how to use a new tool is implementation. But marketing and communicating the *change* (and in particular, the WIIFM for all the different stakeholders)—that's deployment.

Differentiating between deployment and implementation isn't just semantics for the sake of semantics. It's important for organizations to use these terms precisely to ensure that everyone understands what is happening and why. This goes back to that recurring problem of relying too much on technology to do all the heavy lifting for you. Implementation serves to meet the technical requirements of a complex business process, but deployment is what guarantees that this technology is integrated into the rest of your workforce experience strategy and is understood by the workforce as valuable.

Process Design:
Digitization versus Automation

In chapter 1, we described automation as simply taking what we have now and putting it online, while digitization is reimagining something in a way that enhances it technologically *and* adds value to the experience. We should also look at deployment through that automation versus digitization lens, challenging ourselves to actually rethink how each workday process we use can thrive in a world that is now digital. This means asking questions like, "How does information flow to people? How do we personalize information in a way that delivers exactly what employees need, while filtering out the irrelevant stuff? How do we optimize the workflow regimen throughout the organization?"

As an example, let's say our goal is to do away with the rigmarole of getting a supervisor to formally approve a personnel change—which, in the outmoded method of most organizations, usually requires printing out a document, signing it, putting it in the interoffice mail, and waiting for the recipient to get it, sign it, and send it back through the interoffice mail.

"Automation" would be filling out the form via a PDF reader, signing it electronically, and emailing it. That's better, but inadequate. You still have to wait for the official approval to be processed. You still have to use email, which can be cumbersome. In all likelihood, you still have to sign in to one account or another. That's no great tragedy, but every little extra step means more of your day wasted on administrative stuff. It adds up.

"Digitization" would be different—it might be something like enabling all or part of the form to be filled out automatically (using the information that's already in the database), and with a single click on the Submit button routing it automatically to the supervisor who needs to sign off on it. As soon as that person presses Approve, the personnel change is verified and official.

When it comes to *creating an experience* (and not merely implementing a module), practice empathy. Put yourself in others' shoes and imagine how the same technology will function in different contexts. If you're heading workforce technology for a major grocery chain, think about how store clerks are going to engage with the software. On a daily basis, they already deal with twenty other tools and processes conducted on the point-of-sale terminal they use to ring up customers. Wouldn't it be better to integrate workforce experience functionality right there, at the point of sale, using an interface they already know inside out, instead of putting it on some dusty old break-room desktop they can only access a few times a day?

Phase Zero: Before the Beginning

Many organizations botch the deployment of workforce experience programs by rushing headlong into it. Then they quickly realize they're missing certain key components or haven't really thought through their plan. Maybe they've failed to secure cooperation from the necessary departments, or they find that executive oversight (so crucial for success) is absent. As they scramble to fix things, it soon becomes apparent that it's very difficult to bring the train back once it has left the station.

Phase Zero is a term used in industries such as management, pharmacology, and diplomacy, among others. In the context of a workforce experience program, it means taking an inventory of all the materials, schedules, personnel, processes, and technology needed to move from "pre-deployment" into Phase 1 of deployment. It is truly creating the experience architecture for today and into the future. The purpose of the Phase Zero review is obvious: it prevents the kinds of "leaping before you look" logjams that stymie the rollout of major organizational initiatives.

This might seem so intuitive as not to even warrant mention—why would any organization dive into such a massive program before double-checking that all the pieces are in place? But in fact, it happens regularly.

Let's not forget that organizations often don't follow the same logic as individual people. Organizations are collective structures composed of a large number of actors with distinct and sometimes divergent interests, personalities, skills, etc. As a whole, therefore, an organization may not behave like a rational system, even if everyone within the organization is doing their job (and, let's be honest, that in itself is a pretty generous assumption!). This is one reason why organizations sometimes commit head-scratching gaffes that seem, in hindsight, like they could have been easily avoided.

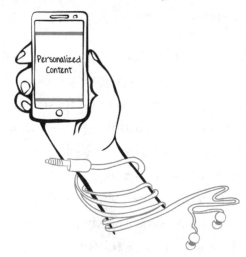

Illustration 24: From Adoption to Addiction

Admit it: we're all hooked. Some are more hopelessly hooked than others, but every one of us is addicted to technology in some form or other. Of course, too much use is a problem, but a little bit of habitual use keeps people engaged with the games, apps, or websites they love. Technology addiction is what fuels a thriving consumer industry, which has perfected the art of self-reinforcing demand: the more you use a given technology or service, the more you seem to crave it. Human resources should respond to this quirk in human nature by encouraging a healthy addiction to the digital workforce experience.

People are often skeptical about the propensity of workers to get "hooked" on this technology—we are, after all, talking about unglamorous HR software. It doesn't have the same habit-forming allure of photo-sharing or gaming or messaging close friends. In reality, we are not going to get them addicted to the technology, but to the experience. You aren't going to get addicted to changing your address, enrolling in direct deposit, or (unless you live a particularly wild life) registering the birth of a new baby.

However, you *can* get hooked on the convenience and novelty of the digital workforce experience as a whole: a one-stop shop where you can find anything you need to do to get your job done, whether it's submitting expense reports with a single click, easily locating a phone number from the sprawling corporate directory, or enrolling in career development courses you didn't even know existed.

Until now, all these tasks have been effectively decentralized. They existed under the HR umbrella generally, but one HR silo handled onboarding, another one took care of employee benefits issues, a third handled talent management, and so forth. Each thing had its own frustratingly unique hoop-jumping process; sometimes it was a challenge just to find the right person to ask how to do something, much less to actually do it.

It was like grocery shopping before the rise of supermarkets (but without any of the mom-and-pop charm): one trip to the butcher to buy meat, one stop at the greengrocer to pick up veggies, a crosstown visit to the pharmacist—adding up to an all-day ordeal just to pick up the basics.

The term *self-service* is often used in connection with the digital workforce experience. Interestingly enough, the now-ubiquitous "self-service" method of putting groceries in your cart was virtually unheard of before supermarkets revamped the industry. In the days of mom-and-pop shopping, you'd hand a clerk a list of your needs, and he'd go fetch those items for you. But once consumers were given the option of walking the aisles and finding products themselves, without the aid of a clerk, they never wanted to go back to the way things had been.

The centralization of everything drives employee "addiction," improves communication (by providing one convenient medium through which to deliver information and services to people), and makes possible the data and feedback collection that powers the whole system. The more people interact with the workforce experience interface, the better it works, creating a self-reinforcing feedback loop.

What we're offering is essentially the digital equivalent of strategically designing retail stores. An entire consumer science is dedicated to fine-tuning a store's layout and product arrangement to boost sales. Sometimes these techniques are subtle, almost subliminal (incorporating "breaks" into long aisles to keep customers' eyes moving, or adding rounded corners, which shoppers find more inviting than hard angles). Other times, the design features are hidden in plain sight. In certain drugstores, for example, you might see a line running along the floor that visually pushes you to follow a certain path. The expectation is that if you follow that line, you'll pass by certain products in a certain order that analysts have determined is ideal for encouraging browsing and buying.

In retail as in the workforce experience, the basic idea is the same: to give the consumer one path to follow as they do their "shopping." If we give them ten different paths at work, we lose control over how they engage with the system, and they get frustrated by the lack of clarity and efficiency. But if we place all the "products" they need within arm's reach along a carefully designed digital path, they'll find what they need quickly and be more inclined to return the next time they need something done. The ease and efficiency of this experience is what drives addiction.

Kick-Start the Habit: Proven Marketing Ideas

Moving from adoption to addiction is, like many other aspects of the digital workforce experience, a long-term project, not a one-and-done situation. It requires constant communication with the target audience over an extended period, and it begins well before the actual launch.

Start by building up buzz through multiple channels, in the same way that film studios promote upcoming releases. Twelve to sixteen weeks before opening weekend, the studios will blanket the media market with a teaser trailer, screening it on TV, in theaters, and on the web, along with other multi-media promo content. If it's a kids' movie or a superhero flick, there might be merchandising deals with a fast-food chain or a toy company.

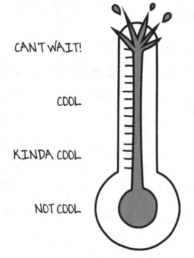

CAN'T WAIT!

COOL

KINDA COOL

NOT COOL

Illustration 25: Building Buzz

There are dozens of other sources of entertainment competing for the consumer's attention (and their dollar), but the studios hope that after weeks of exposure through multiple channels, the movie will have seeped into the public consciousness by the time of the premiere. People talk about it, pass it around on social media, "sell" the movie to each other, spiking demand by the time the film debuts.

Likewise, in your organization, you should start the buzz-building campaign weeks or months before the launch date so that people will be halfway addicted before they even see the new workforce experience. You want to reveal enough to entice them, but not so much that you kill the mystique, just as the production companies do. After all, they don't call it a "*teaser* trailer" for nothing.

It's also useful to have a group of change champions spread throughout the organization: people who are incented to turn their peers on to the new technology. The incentive can be extra time off, credit at the company store, a restaurant gift card—whatever works. Some of these change champions will be employees who were involved in the earlier stages of planning the workforce experience program. Others may have been uninvolved until now. Look for those who tend to be noisy about their desires and those who wield social influence among their colleagues. These individuals usually make effective change agents.

Consider other time-tested marketing techniques, too, such as contests—maybe the first X number of people who use the new workforce experience platform get a prize. I once worked at a firm where the first five hundred people to enroll in online benefits were awarded a sweatshirt. I did not win. And did I feel a twinge of envy every time I saw one of my colleagues walking around in that sweatshirt? You bet. Never underestimate the power of friendly competition to ignite people's passions.

Another method: embed "Easter eggs" into the technology, hiding little digital treasures for users to find. Any kind of gamification will generate interest and get people excited about something they might otherwise find a bit humdrum. After all, everyone loves a treasure hunt!

In addition to these ideas, you can fall back on more conventional methods of getting the word out. Not everything has to be a flashy marketing gimmick. One effective technique is to set aside a few minutes of management meetings to "train the trainers." Give managers a crash course in how to engage with the new system so that they can pass that knowledge on to employees.

The important thing is that now that there's a self-service module in place, which, you need to remember, is not what we call it outside of HR, managers and HR personnel will no longer be burdened by the administrative issues they used to have to handle. This requires a kind of "forced abstinence." Naturally, there will be a learning curve and perhaps a few grumbles along the way as everyone adjusts from the old system to the new. But once they see the benefits for themselves—once they *experience* them—they'll never want to go back to how things were before.

TAKEAWAYS

1. **Prioritize your responsibilities.**

   Prioritization is not as simple as just doing the most important things first. Sometimes, seemingly minor tasks take precedence because they help set up more significant components later. An urgency-impact matrix helps you organize and visualize the myriad tasks that require your attention.

2. **Before deploying, run a thorough "Phase Zero" check.**

   Preventing crises is always preferable to dealing with them after they've emerged during a busy rollout. Don't rush: before you go live, make sure that the mindset, people, processes, and technologies required for the new workforce experience program are in place.

3. **Encourage the transition from adoption to addiction.**

   "Adoption" means your customers are using a new system because they have to. "Addiction" means they're using it because they *want* to. Once you've reached the addiction phase, the program has self-sustaining momentum. But that doesn't mean you can rest just yet, because . . .

4. **Marketing is as important now as ever.**

   Start building buzz well before you go live, and continue doing so once the program is launched. When it comes to digital technology, novelty has a short shelf life: what feels fresh today is old hat tomorrow. Continue promoting aspects of the program and rolling out new features to keep that spark alive.

ROI: Run, Optimize, Innovate

If you're a parent, it's something you'll never forget: that moment when you bring your newborn home from the hospital and gaze down lovingly at this mewling, doe-eyed little thing. It fills you with a heady mix of awe, trepidation, affection, bewilderment—and probably a mild to acute sense of panic, now that the full weight of your new lifetime responsibility begins to dawn on you.

The pregnancy was a roller-coaster ride, and you were so caught up in getting ready for the birth that you scarcely had a chance to think about what would come next. Well, after nine months of planning and prep, now you've "gone live" (quite literally!) with this baby. Undoubtedly, you've got your work cut out for you, for a long, long time—nothing is more perpetual beta than a human being. But you're thrilled.

Illustration 26: "Go Begin" Onesie

There are a lot of parallels between birthing a baby and launching a digital workforce experience program—and I don't mean just the sleepless nights and hormonal rage. For one, the "birth" of a workforce experience is when the fun starts, when the hard work starts paying off, when you and others can see the value that it brings, and when you can prove to your colleagues the merit of what you have been laboring over all this time. But as any new parent will tell you, the launch initiates a new phase that requires an entirely different set of skills.

Emphasizing the Value

In the early days, the just-debuted workforce experience program is fresh in everyone's minds, and you can use this to your advantage. The mic is live; the stage is yours; all eyes are on you. This kind of moment is so valuable in large organizations, where at any given point so many different things are competing for employees' attention. Make sure you tout the initial successes of the program by showing how it's adding value from Day 1.

First, look at the emotional benefit. The beauty of the digital workforce experience is that at its heart, it's a very human, touchy-feely initiative. Celebrating moments that matter is an important theme of the workforce experience, and the first few days and weeks after going live provide a special opportunity to place those moments in the spotlight. Find a way to recognize the first ten or fifteen people who have a great experience with the new program as a way of showing others how they, too, can benefit.

For example, imagine that employees have always been frustrated by the process of calling the HR service desk. One of the new features you've just rolled out replaces that process with a self-service, point-and-click module, along with a 24/7 chatbot for users who need extra help. Users will generate feedback that expresses their satisfaction with the new system and their gratitude that they no longer have to play phone tag to obtain the answer to a simple question.

I've seen it many times: at first, employees are tentative as they adjust to the change, but in a matter of days or weeks, they take to it. As the feedback trickles in, you'll hear things like, "Wow, that was great. For the first time, I could actually get the help I needed. It felt as easy as shopping online. It felt like the organization cares about my needs." That kind of testimonial encapsulates the emotional content of the experience. It's what resonates with people and turns new users on to the system. Emotion is the essence of an experience of any kind.

We can gauge this sentiment not just through words, but through numbers as well. One useful metric is the "net promoter score," which asks questions like, "Would you recommend this process to your peers?" The net promoter score is usually tabulated via a smile sheet on which users indicate their opinion by selecting a happy face, neutral face, or sad face (or, in technical terms, "detractor," "passive," or "promoter"). It's an easy, straightforward metric that provides a snapshot of the overall health of a given process or tool.

In addition to emotional rewards, the other primary benefit of the workforce experience program is more business-oriented— simply put, it will save the organization money by increasing efficiency, cutting HR-related costs, and freeing up extra hours of labor, which all translate into a productivity boost.

The aforementioned example talked about the emotional value of eliminating the headache of calling a help desk, but such an improvement has a clear cost-cutting advantage, too. And the new workforce experience's powerful data architecture empowers you to statistically analyze the impact on various human-resources–related functions with a high level of precision.

For instance, if we've digitized the customer service process with the goal of reducing help-desk call volume, and we see that after four weeks, incoming calls have declined by 33 percent, then we can easily calculate the impact on the bottom line (given that every shared service call costs an organization fifty to seventy-five dollars, on average).

Finally, when communicating the value of the new program, don't just look at its current value; keep building excitement for the potential future value. Talk about what you're going to do next. Extend the buzz-building that began before you rolled out the program. Even after going live, you want people to keep coming back for more; you want to prolong that initial burst of enthusiasm, which is what facilitates the transition from adoption to addiction. This means unveiling new features and new functions as the weeks go on.

The sooner you can demonstrate the value of the workforce experience, the more likely you are to secure its future. This is no time to rest on your laurels. In many organizations, competition for funds is a never-ending battle, and if you can't demonstrate the tangible benefit of your initiative, it might end up on the chopping block. If the company endures a rough quarter, an overzealous auditor casts a skeptical eye in your direction, or a new executive comes in who wasn't involved in the planning and doesn't understand what a digital workforce experience is, the entire program you've worked so hard to build could be in jeopardy.

The burden is on us to prove its value from the start and show that it pays for itself by boosting morale, saving time and money, and keeping people loyal and engaged.

Optimize: Skill-Set Shift

A special set of skills is needed once everything is up and running. The type of person needed to plan and deploy something is different from the type of person needed to keep the program healthy and growing. It's one thing to go live; it's quite another to sustain and expand upon that initial success.

The digital workforce experience is not static; it's a living, breathing organism, and it needs to be fed and nurtured to grow. We look at what we have, and we think every day about how to make it better, not by gussying up the things we've done in the past, but by designing our processes differently.

That's really all that *optimizing* means: continually adding value. One way is by debuting new features according to the rollout calendar that we set up before going live. The other way is by coming up with new ideas on the fly as we examine how the program develops, how people use it, what's popular, what's underutilized (or loathed), and what needs to change.

Continuous **Improvement**

Illustration 27: Continuous Improvement Superman

Because we've built a strong data foundation that generates constant feedback, we have a never-ending supply of information to inspire our next move. It all ties back into our vision, and into the simple but fundamental question, "What are we doing on an everyday basis to make the stuff that we put out there better?"

For that reason, one of the critical post-rollout skills we need to cultivate is analytics. And not just analytics in the traditional sense, but analytics tied to experience. That requires truly understanding where the program is working and, if it's breaking down, how to triage that quickly by utilizing feedback loops to gauge user sentiment and feeding that information back into the system to refine it. One reason analytics has been poorly or inadequately applied to the human resources profession is because our data has been incomplete. The dark days of bad data are done—but we need people who are proficient in analytics so that we can take advantage of the change.

In addition, we need dedicated marketing people in HR to continue promoting the program, teaching people how to use it, and communicating new benefits and features.

In truth, employees have always poorly understood what we in HR really do all day long. They know we deal with payroll, recruitment, and benefits, but in their eyes, the benefits HR provides them day in and day out are opaque. At best, we've been that coterie of paper-pushing eggheads who know way too much about the finer points of matching 401(k) contributions; at worst, we're seen as some kind of corporate police, charged with enforcing the rules and cracking down when people don't do things by the book.

It's unfortunate that such misconceptions have muddled the perception of our purpose, but HR professionals own a lot of the blame for this, since we've never really been good at marketing ourselves. (If we were, we'd probably be working down the hall in the marketing department.) We've never quite found our voice when it comes to effectively communicating our own role in the organization, and especially around our raison d'être: that we are not workforce watchdogs, but we are simply trying to make working there better.

Marketing, analytics, sentiment analysis: "When did I sign up for all this?" you might ask. But in applying these new skills to our own profession, we don't need to start at the very beginning. This has all been done already in other disciplines. If you're at a loss about how to learn, go to your marketing or sales departments, because they've been doing it for years. Now it's our turn.

Illustration 28: Prescription

Innovate: It's a Sprint, Not a Marathon

In the past, HR has dealt with problems with all the urgency of a glacier. Whether from lack of will, dearth of technical capacity, or just because that was how we were accustomed to doing things, if there was a minor problem, we'd usually wait until "the next release" or "the following phase" to resolve it. That might mean it wouldn't be fixed for another six months.

Illustration 29: Sprint vs. Marathon

With the digital workforce experience in place, we're running a series of short sprints rather than one long marathon. We're living in an era of agile design and agile execution, tackling technical problems rapidly and with surgical precision. If our data tells us that 65 percent of users are abandoning a given process halfway though, we can address it right away. Gone is the time of collecting complaints for four months, going into a protracted development mode, pushing out a solution a few months later, and then disappearing back into our hole for another four months until the maddening cycle starts anew.

Here is a situation I encountered recently. One organization was being bombarded with confused calls from employees whose paychecks were printed with "BNS: $300.00" or "BNS: $450.00." BNS was just a payroll code for "bonus"—but who outside of HR would know that?

Instead of waiting months to fix this simple problem, today, we have the right data and the right processes to tackle it right away, just by changing the wording from "BNS" to "Bonus," and thus ending the volley of calls. The outcome is a win-win-win: the organization cuts down on help-desk costs; the HR staff is relieved of the burden of explaining the same thing over and over; and the employees can finally understand their own paycheck. It's the little things, like sparing workers an extra dose of confusion on payday, when they're getting ready to knock off for the weekend, that make an organization a pleasant place to be.

Running sprints mandates that we continue to think innovatively. Innovation just means making changes to something established by introducing new methods, ideas, or products. How can we continue to make things better? How can we integrate the feedback (positive as well as negative) from employees and use it to refine our tools and processes?

HR departments tend to be so busy fighting fires and keeping the lights on that we've overlooked—or maybe just haven't had time for—innovation. Now that digitization can systematize certain tasks that have consumed so much of our workday, we have more time to think strategically and creatively. That is really where our true value to the organization begins, and it's an area where we're just beginning to scratch the surface. This development opens up a new realm of possibilities for the profession as a whole.

Illustration 30: Plan

Governance: Keeping It All Together

Governance can seem like an unpleasant word, connoting enforcement, regulation, compliance, monitoring, and other things that employees tend to resent. But when we talk of governance in the context of a workforce experience, it just means adhering to a standardized set of aesthetic and practical norms. The workforce experience program should look and feel uniform from top to bottom, rather than being a hodgepodge of styles and functionalities.

Employees rely on the workforce experience interface for multiple HR-related issues. In the span of a single hour, someone might want to enroll in health benefits, look up the policy on bringing pets to work, and submit an overdue expense report. Doing so should be seamless; that is, the interface should feel like one unified system, even as they wade through all these disparate issues. The design should be standardized, the different processes should be similar, and the mechanism for navigating different parts of the interface should be consistent. It should not feel like you're walking down Main Street, but when you turn a corner, you find yourself in the middle of the Amazon rainforest.

Or, to continue the analogy from the previous chapter, when you enter a supermarket, you can see immediately that there is a uniformity of design, style, and layout that ties every section of the store under one brand. The dairy aisle, the spice aisle, and the deli have a cohesive look, even though the products are different.

Now, obviously, the challenge of governance is that the workforce experience itself is diverse, holistic, cross-departmental, and multifunctional. How do we keep such a multifaceted thing uniform? The key is to make sure the governance group is itself cross-functional and includes people from HR, IT, the C-suite, people involved in the actual business of the company, and everyone else who has a stake in its success. Give each stakeholder room to play and create and innovate, but do so within the confines of an agreed-upon structure.

Besides managing and monitoring standards, another important function of the governance group is coordinating the rollout of new tools. Obviously, you don't want to bombard the workforce with too many new features in too short a time; nor do you want to wait forever before unveiling the next thing. There should be a certain rhythm to how you add tools and perks, and the only way to achieve that is to make sure all the groups are coordinating with each other on when and where to do so.

Measuring Your ROI

ROI is an apt term to describe this phase of developing a digital workforce experience because of its dual meanings: "run, optimize, innovate," and the more familiar "return on investment," when organizations begin to see that the workforce experience is producing results. The two meanings are inextricably linked: organizations achieve their best ROI when they remain active and engaged, always striving to optimize and improve upon it rather than just letting it sit there.

And for HR people, this opens up new opportunities to really focus on where we shine. Since workforce experience technology can now shoulder more of the day-to-day, keeping-the-lights-on banalities, we can devote more attention to specialized, innovative, strategic tasks.

In fact, we're witnessing a seismic shift in the HR profession itself. In the next chapter, we'll look at what the future might bring—and talk about how it's bearing down on us faster than we think.

TAKEAWAYS

1. Continuous improvement means rapid solutions.

The dominance of digital and mobile technologies demands that problems are solved with speed, agility, and a minimum of red tape. If something isn't working, we can no longer bounce the problem around among multiple working groups for months, or view it as an internal, HR-specific problem. Now that technology has been turned inside out, such that the average worker interacts with HR-related software every day, we have to be more diligent about fixing problems as soon as they arise.

2. Showcase the value.

Most of the visible benefits of the workforce experience will be either emotional (making employees feel better on the job) or financial (cutting costs and increasing productivity). Talk to employees and analyze the data to find out where the program is working best. Share these early triumphs with everyone. Doing so will expedite the transition from adoption to addiction as more people use it, and it will cement the workforce experience as a permanent fixture of the organization once the higher-ups see it adds value.

3. Deepen your existing skills, but continue to hone new ones.

Certain skills are more important after the launch than prior to it. The organization will need a workforce experience team with analytics chops, marketing prowess, and a talent for innovation and optimization. Some of these skills lie outside our normal area of expertise, but if we can broaden our repertoire, everyone benefits.

4. Keep everything uniform.

Good governance ensures consistency of form and function. The workforce experience should look and feel like a well-designed store: intuitive to browse, aesthetically clean, and with all components adhering to a clear layout—a brand, really. Make sure your governance group is multifunctional and multi-departmental to keep everyone on the same page.

10

The Future (Is Today)

I have good news and bad news. Let's start with the bad news: the future is here already. We don't have the luxury of slow, careful deliberation. There's no time to get our feet wet or test the waters—the wave of change is cresting over us. Digital technology has already completely reinvented how people engage with the world, and its reach is only going to expand. HR professionals need to adapt—or we risk fading into irrelevance, and you may be thinking you are at this point in the book.

Illustration 31: Dive, Not Tip-Toe

Now for the good news, which happens to be the same as the bad: the future is here already. The rise of mobile, big data, AI, the consumerization of the workplace, and all the other interrelated trends that affect how we live, work, and play offer a once-in-a-generation chance to reinvent the experience of work—and to reinvent ourselves as HR professionals in the process.

The Future of People

When it comes to people, there are two groups we need to think about: the workforce itself and human resources personnel.

Current well-established employment trends will only become more pervasive in the coming years: more people working remotely, the expansion of flexible labor and the gig economy, a higher degree of global interconnectedness, the continued digitization of everything, and an influx of digital natives—who have grown up online—entering the workforce.

As a result of these trends, the workforce of the future will look different from the one we're used to, and since employees are our customers, we need to think differently about how we'll serve them. What kind of experience will the next generation want at work?

To deliver what they desire, we need to get better at practicing empathy and operating from an outside-in, workforce-centric paradigm. This development, along with technological pressures I'll address in this chapter, is going to reshape our day-to-day responsibilities, as the focus of human resources management moves beyond an emphasis on answering questions to a focus on solving problems.

Illustration 32: Answering Questions

The more artificial intelligence, machine learning, and related technologies advance, the greater the number of tasks that will fall under the umbrella of RAD (repeatable, auditable, and documented). Bots might handle some things adeptly, but they are not designed to deal with certain critical HR issues—namely, problems that are emotional, personal, and situation-specific. If an employee experiences a death in the family, or a tragedy has struck at work, a bot cannot provide grief counseling, advise about bereavement leave, or provide psychological comfort in a difficult time. That level of AI sophistication is still confined to the realm of science fiction—and even if such technology were theoretically feasible, would grieving people want to consult with or be consoled by a robot?

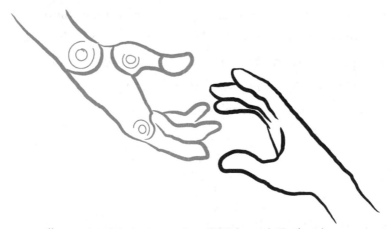

Illustration 33: Augmenting People with Technology

It is these situations—these *moments that matter*, the good as well as the bad—that remind us how essential our role is, even as technology plays an increasingly dominant part in our line of work.

The Future of Process

Every process that affects how people work needs to be reinvented or reimagined: turned inside out, upside down, and, as always, designed with the workforce at the center rather than as an afterthought.

Historically, consumer-facing industries have always been on the forefront of process innovation, with HR following suit. We must be diligent about staying on top of these changes and adopting them as needed—keeping up with the rest of the world, in other words. How do people communicate with their bank? How do people communicate with their airline? How do people communicate with each other? Do they want to call a hotline to lodge a complaint, or do they get faster results from venting on social media? What can we learn from the titans of the tech industry? What are they doing that might work well in our own workplace, and what can we safely ignore?

In other words, how can we rethink these processes to embed them into a frictionless workforce experience? And how can we do that in a way that fulfills the long-term vision of the HR department as a problem solver rather than a question answerer?

If an employee wants to request time off, that process should be as simple and intuitive as pouring a glass of water from the tap. No instruction should be necessary; it's just there. You just *do it*. In that respect, the challenge of the future is not really about making processes easy to learn. We want to design processes with as short a learning curve as possible.

New processes should be seamlessly integrated with technologies that people use every day. Instead of calling HR about vacation accrual, employees should be able to ask Siri or Alexa what the policy is. Instead of having to log in to an account and click through a bunch of screens to view one's paycheck, the paycheck should automatically be delivered weekly to the employee's smartphone. If there's a payroll problem, we shouldn't make people figure out whom to call, or make them navigate through a jungle of links and buttons; just let them click on the paycheck and speak directly with someone who can resolve it. Then, if the problem can't be fixed immediately, give the employee a case number so they can track the progress as easily as Domino's customers can follow the path of their pizza delivery.

Here's a key point to remember: the future of the process is the conversation. You will be designing conversations that personalize the feel to the workforce and bring humanity into the life of your processes. Hold on to your hats for those still struggling with process design; this is about to get fun!

The Future of Technology

Even I'm sometimes blown away by how much workforce technology has advanced. These days, talking to a chatbot can feel so smooth and natural that you wonder if there really isn't a human being on the other end. And five years from now, chatbots are going to be able to do a lot more than answer questions. They're going to be smarter, have the capacity to "learn," and be able to solve problems—not just react in response to a question, but be predictive and prescriptive.

Within the next few years, AI will be adapted to many other HR-related functions, continuing the trend of letting machines handle an increasingly specialized array of tasks. Headless apps, which lack a graphical user interface, are another promising tool for the future.

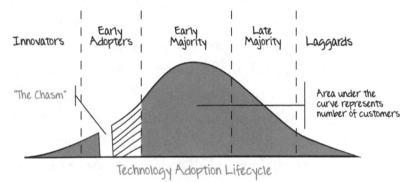

Illustration 33: Technology Adoption Lifecycle

When it comes to these "new" technologies, we're really at the border between innovation and adoption, that phase when novel types of software and hardware go from state-of-the-art to status quo. Just as we don't really talk about mobile technology as new anymore, I predict that in a few years, we're no longer going to think of AI and bots as new, but as the norm. This is both exciting and disconcerting. We've known this day would come, and yet, now that it's dawning, it all feels like it's happening at breakneck speed.

Regardless of what we do with disruptive technologies that enter the market, we should continue to follow the paradigm that technology be molded to users and not vice versa—that the user must adapt to the technology. That means personalization, ease of use, automation, and other hallmarks of a frictionless experience that delivers the right service to the right people through the right channel at the right time.

Hence, the "spray and pray" approach to HR technology, where we throw a bunch of stuff at the wall and see what sticks, is on a path toward obsolescence. Because we're approaching the human resources role through a more empathetic lens, and because we can now gather and analyze data in staggeringly powerful ways, we understand who our employees are better than ever before. And by taking this deep, broad knowledge of the workforce and linking it with design thinking, we can do things differently, better, more precisely, and more seamlessly.

As always, the workforce experience we end up creating will depend on the kind of technology the users want. If people prefer talking into a device rather than navigating around menus, we'll develop our tools accordingly. If people are partial to doing things on their desktop because that's where they spend 90 percent of their day, we're going to let them interact with desktop applications. Whatever our approach is going forward, it should feel natural for the user and be tailored to the user's needs and wants.

Throughout this book, we've talked a lot about the consumerization of human resources: adapting to the workplace the processes and technology that make the consumer experience such a breeze. However, there is a little more nuance to it; it's not just as simple as using Apple or Samsung as a benchmark. The technologies we implement must fit *our* employees' needs.

Digitize strategically; don't just try to keep up with the Joneses.

In the past, we were stymied by the technology, or lack thereof. It seemed that we had to plan everything around the next iteration of a piece of software—or in some cases, the available technology just didn't allow us to do what we envisioned. Today, we have all the technology at our fingertips that we could ever need. What we haven't done is get the people and process components down and figure out how best to leverage that technology. That will be one of the bigger challenges of the future.

The Future Ain't What It Used to Be

For most organizations, thinking ahead means having plans for how they're going to upgrade to the next version of their software, handle updates from a cloud vendor, or implement the latest talent management platform. But very few organizations have a holistic plan that addresses these fundamental questions: "How are we going reskill the HR function? How will we change how we deliver services? How will we leverage future technologies in accord with a durable long-term version?" Without thinking and acting holistically, organizations are just throwing money away and setting themselves up for bigger problems down the road.

All these questions raise even more issues: what is our own future identity as human resources professionals? Where do we fit in within our company, our industry, the economy, society at large? What is our purpose? What is our role?

At present, HR is going through an awkward adolescent phase, when we're trying to come to grips with developments beyond our control as we assert our presence in a changing economy. Like adolescence, it's a sometimes messy, confusing process of discarding the old and welcoming the new as we grow and mature, as we stake a claim to our identity and figure out where we stand in this brave new world.

The future is here already, and our profession is at a pivotal moment. The rate of change (technologically, economically, and culturally) is ever-increasing, making it harder and harder to keep up. And I expect that in a few years, many organizations will face an AI crisis that we will be forced to reckon with, whether we are ready for it or not. In a few decades, we've gone from the mainframe to DOS to Windows to client server to the web. Through five generations of technology, we've really been doing the same thing, just using new products. AI is fundamentally different. It's not just doing the same thing with a new piece of software or hardware. It's actually changing the way we work, putting the trust of our manual heroics that have defined HR for decades into the bits and bytes of a machine.

Others seem to be better prepared for the dawning AI revolution. Enterprises are ready, vendors are ready, workers are ready, but many people in HR are still clinging to convention, or so fixated on their day-to-day responsibilities that they're not looking at the horizon, or perhaps they are too worried that chatbots are going to take their jobs.

Displacement by automation is a valid concern, and it has indeed put people out of work in other sectors, but in HR, those fears are largely unfounded. The future we face (if we are brave enough to face it) is not tech-induced redundancy, but the reskilling of our profession: becoming more strategic and more innovative—less question-answering, more problem-solving. That means using the data foundation to address critical issues like how many people we will need to hire in the future and which skills will be in demand. It means having a seat at the table to help with business strategy—to know exactly what personnel needs the firm will face when it undergoes an ambitious international expansion, or to figure out a brilliant way to optimize labor resources when the company is struggling and needs to fortify the bottom line.

Changes are coming, but we can't merely sit back and wait for them to arrive. Enterprises move fast today, and it's only a matter of time before the CEO of your firm comes back from a conference where he's dazzled by all the eye-popping things his peers are doing with artificial intelligence and says, "Hey, HR, why aren't we doing that here?" We have to plan for it. Otherwise, by remaining inert, we're building a technical debt that we'll have to scramble to pay back as we play catch-up. I've heard many questionable excuses for putting it off, but the most frequent might be, "We're moving in that direction, but we don't have that project teed up for this year." Sorry, but this is not a project. This is your job!

So, there is indeed a real sense of urgency we should be mindful of—not because robots will take our jobs, but because if we don't adapt to the way the world works, the way *work* works, we won't be able to adequately serve our employees and our organizations—which is the very reason we exist. HR shouldn't devolve into a dinosaur department of people who do data entry; instead, we're the ones who should lead the charge into the next phase of the digital age, proudly and confidently affirming our emerging role as strategists and innovators.

The technological revolution can be both daunting and exhilarating. But it's clear to me from the organizations I've worked with around the world that those that embrace the changes will be most successful. Human resources management will never be replaced by bots. Humans aren't machines.

Humans have issues that, unlike machines, will always require the intelligence, nuance, and emotional acumen of people to resolve. It's one of the things we relish about our profession.

We love that this is a think-on-your-feet kind of job that demands continuous improvement. So, let's improve. The world of managing, leading, and dealing with people is never going to vanish. Not at all. We're only just getting started.

TAKEAWAYS

1. The workforce is changing, and we must change with it.

Remote work, an evolving workplace culture, borderlessness, and other such trends are reshaping how people work. Our workforce experience strategy should evolve accordingly.

2. Create processes (and conversations) that are designed with the workforce in mind.

No matter what staggering changes await us, one constant will remain: we must meet the members of the workforce where they are, letting them work how they want, with the tools and processes they desire. It is an expansion of the outside-in, workforce-centric design thinking that is already emerging in HR.

3. Technology won't push us out the door—but we can't sit idle, either.

Digitization is only a threat to our livelihoods if we fail to plan for it. We must develop a vision for the future that is strategic, rather than just scheduling the next software upgrade. HR must also prepare by reskilling the profession so that we can continue to provide value to organizations in a world driven by mobile, digital, and AI.

4. We are straddling the border between present and future.

The future is here already. It's a strange moment, but a unique opportunity. We are fortunate that we still have